Fisherfolk of Charlotte Harbor, Florida

Fisherfolk of Charlotte Harbor, Florida

by Robert F. Edic

Institute of Archaeology and
Paleoenvironmental Studies

University of Florida

Gainesville

1996

The University of Florida Institute of Archaeology and Paleoenvironmental Studies gratefully acknowledges the assistance of the Bureau of Historic Preservation, Division of Historical Resources, Florida Department of State in the publication of this book. However, the contents and opinions do not necessarily reflect the views and opinions of the Florida Department of State, nor does the mention of trade names or commercial products constitute endorsement or recommendation by the Florida Department of State.

Printed in Canada

Institute of Archaeology and Paleoenvironmental Studies
Florida Museum of Natural History
P.O. Box 117800, University of Florida
Gainesville, Florida 32611-7800 U.S.A.

Library of Congress Cataloging-in-Publication Data

Edic, Robert F. (Robert Franklin), 1945-
    Fisherfolk of Charlotte Harbor, Florida / by Robert F. Edic.
      p.   cm.
    Includes bibliographical references (p.   ) and index.
    ISBN 1-881448-04-5 (pbk. : alk. paper)
    1. Fisheries--Florida--Charlotte Harbor Region (Bay)--History.
2. Charlotte Harbor (Fla. : Bay)--History. 3. Fishers--Florida--
Charlotte Harbor Region (Bay)--Interviews. I. Title.
SH222.F6E35 1996
305.9'6392'097594--dc20   95-33684
                                       CIP

Design by Alice Allen
Cover design by Claudine Payne

Cover photograph: Members of

Coleman and Padilla families off to visit

relatives, circa 1920s.

(Photo courtesy of Richard Coleman.)

Tom Parkinson at Boca Grande Fishery, circa 1985. (Photo courtesy of Boca Beacon.*)*

Dedication

This book is dedicated to

Thomas S. Parkinson: a man in command of the

knowledge of years lived and with humanity

from which we can all learn.

Contents

Foreword

It was 1984 when I first met Bob Edic. I was researching the archaeology of the Calusa Indians, ancient inhabitants of Charlotte Harbor. Bob had been collecting oral histories with today's senior fisherfolk. As Bob and I talked, I realized that these men and women had in their youth fished the waters of Charlotte Harbor much as the ancient Calusa Indians had — without today's monofilament nets, motorboats, and ice, and in an undeveloped and unpolluted environment quite different from that of today.

I began to pepper Bob with questions. What was it like to net-fish before monofilament and motorboats? How had storms and red tides affected early twentieth-century net fishers? What fish were netted, and which ones were caught with hand lines? In what ways had the harbor changed over the past 50 years? "I'll ask them," he said.

The result is this book, but it is far more than the answers to an archaeologist's questions. It is also a personal, often poignant account of one of Florida's oldest industries, one that is rapidly vanishing.

William H. Marquardt
Curator in Archaeology
Florida Museum of Natural History

A train arrives at Gasparilla Village circa 1920s bringing ice from the mainland and picking up passengers and fish packed fresh for shipment north (note the fish house on the right). This train and conveniences such as the IGA store (on left) owned by Gus Cole and a post office ended much of the isolation of the fisherfolk living on Gasparilla Island.

(Photo courtesy of Eunice Albritton.)

Preface

This book records the vanishing fishing traditions of Florida's Charlotte Harbor fisherfolk. Senior fisherfolk of Charlotte Harbor tell in their own words what it was like to fish using methods that may have been handed down from Spanish Cubans, the Calusa Indians, and earlier cultures.

William Marquardt, Ph.D. and Michael Moseley, Ph.D. of the Florida Museum of Natural History and the University of Florida's Department of Anthropology created the University of Florida Institute of Archaeology and Paleoenvironmental Studies (UFIAPS) in 1985 in response to the vandalism on

Grandma Joiner

Effie Melina (Sapp) Joiner was born in 1900 in Manatee County, Florida. She was one of the first and last residents of the historic fishing community known as Gasparilla Village. Most of her seven children were born there. Affectionately known locally as "Grandma" Joiner, she now resides in Boca Grande, Florida. I first met her at Whidden's Marina, where my children spent much of their time under her watchful eyes. Seen here in 1994, she was reviewing pictures I had found of Gasparilla Village during the 1920s. (Photo by Bob Edic.)

Big Mound Key and other sites of archaeological significance in the area. The Southwest Florida Project, a project of the UFIAPS under the direction of Dr. Marquardt, provided assistance in 1987 for the collection of fisherfolk oral histories.

In 1989 the Southwest Florida Project received part of a Special Category Grant from the Bureau of Historic Preservation, Florida Department of State. "The Year of the Indian: Archaeology of the Calusa People" was an archaeological and public education project in cooperation with the Calusa Nature Center and Planetarium, the Fort Myers Historical Museum, and the Lee County Schools.

During 1990 and 1992, education coordinator for "The Year of the Indian" project Charles Blanchard and I organized and trained over six hundred Lee County school teachers in local archaeology. In addition, more than five thousand students received hands-on classroom demonstrations and field trips to the Pineland archaeological site. The project funded the collection of oral histories with senior fisherfolk to gain a better understanding of historic and perhaps prehistoric fishing practices. The University of Florida's Oral History Program under the direction of Samuel Proctor, Ph.D., provided guidance in the collection and transcription of many interviews. Complete transcripts are archived as part of The Florida

Fisherfolk Project and are available for further research in the Oral History Archives, Special Collections, George Smathers Library, University of Florida, Gainesville. In 1992, through funding provided by Oscar and Barbara Hollenbeck and a matching grant from the IBM Corporation to support the fishing heritage research, I was able to compile the oral histories for this book. Grants from the National Endowment for the Humanities; the Maple Hill Foundation; the Ruth and Vernon Taylor Foundation; and the Florida Department of State, Division of Historical Resources, Bureau of Historic Preservation provided funds for editing and publication. I would like to thank Alice Allen for her editing and book design, and Claudine Payne for the cover design.

I would like to thank William Marquardt, Ph.D., and Karen Walker, Ph.D., of the Florida Museum of Natural History for their help. Special thanks also go to Betty Anholt, Charles Blanchard, Merald Clark, Sue Ellen Hunter, Barry Kass, George Luer, Charles Thomas, and to my family—Linda, Dennis, and Darlene—who made it all possible.

Bob Edic
Boca Grande, Florida
November, 1995

Gulf view from the camp site on Cole Island, 1980, where the Edics lived during their first winters in southwest Florida. (Photo by Bob Edic.)

CHAPTER 1

Personal Perspectives

The Edic family—Bob and Linda (rear), Darlene and Dennis, and Dobber (front) on one of our early trips to southwest Florida in the 1970s. (Photo by Jay Browand.)

years, as evidenced by the many large Native American mounds there.

Each day about one thousand people take up residence in Florida, while fewer than two hundred leave. Population growth is, in effect, destroying the very resources that attract so many people in the first place. Managing environmental issues caused by this immigration will, in large part, determine the quality of Florida's future.

Many tourists who visit southwest Florida for the first time view its natural and cultural resources as pristine and unchanged through time. They do not realize that the coconut trees and Seminole Indians, like themselves, are relatively recent arrivals. Tourists are usually unfamiliar with the area's natural history and the different peoples who have altered local environments. In the Charlotte Harbor area, humans have affected plants, animals, water quality, and the landscape itself. Exploitation of rich marine resources has shaped the landscape for at least the past six thousand

Today the inhabitants around the Charlotte Harbor coast are altering their environment in ways that negatively affect the water quality in the area. As a result, southwest Florida's fishery resources are in danger of being lost, and their preservation may depend on an understanding of how their present condition developed.

My family and I were attracted to southwest Florida in 1978. Lured by its apparently perfect coastal environment, I quickly became intrigued with remnants of prehistoric maritime cultures as well as the modern fisheries in the Charlotte Harbor area. Learning about these fishing cultures made it apparent that a lush estuarine environment might be in danger.

Throughout southwest Florida, internationally significant archaeological sites remained unstudied. As I watched, many were being destroyed by treasure hunters, development, and erosion. I was appalled by the disre-

This color infrared photograph was taken of Big Mound Key by Robert Pelham in 1975 for Mote Marine Laboratory. I transferred this to ASA 400 black and white film to expose its unique shape. (Reproduced by permission.)

gard for valuable, non-renewable resources and became involved in efforts to recognize and protect these areas, which were quickly changing because of rapid population growth. Archaeological sites were vanishing at an alarming rate. The only record of preco-

lumbian maritime cultures, other Native American groups, and European pioneers who fished these waters was in jeopardy.

In 1980 treasure hunters had gained access to Big Mound Key, a remote, state-owned archaeological site in Charlotte Harbor on the Cape Haze Peninsula. Wayne Joiner, a friend and local fisherman, guided me to the site soon after the destruction.

Wayne Joiner "poles" through Bull Bay. (Photo by Bob Edic.)

In 1981 archaeologist Calvin Jones (far right) with the Florida Division of Historical Resources inspected the damage done by treasure hunters to Big Mound Key in Charlotte Harbor. Note bulldozer cut through center of mound. From left to right are Steve Botcho, Bob Edic, and Wayne Joiner. (Photo courtesy of Boca Beacon.)

Using heavy bulldozers, the treasure hunters had constructed a road several miles long across state wetlands. They had dissected the site in a number of places with long, deep cuts. The sheer walls of strata left behind revealed the chronology of the peoples who had occupied the harbor for thousands of years.

As an anthropologist, I was intrigued by the evidence the vandalism had made visible. Ronald Fraser and the late Marnie Banks, publisher of the *Boca Beacon*, a local newspaper, helped us inform local and state officials of the damage to the site and the need for salvage archaeology and protection. Archaeologist Calvin Jones from Florida's Division of Historical Resources requested that we begin making surface collections from the damaged areas. I completed "A Preliminary Survey of Big Mound Key" (Edic 1982).

We met George Luer and Marion Almy, local archaeologists also concerned with the damage to Big Mound Key. Together we formed The Mound Foundation, a not-for-profit corporation, to inform the public about the cultural resources being destroyed and to gain protection mandated by law. George Luer's report, "Archaeological Salvage of the Big Mound Key Site," described stratification and thirty-one carbon-14-dated samples from damaged areas (Luer 1982).

Using Big Mound Key artifacts, a small museum was started at the Boca Grande Community House for public education. We lectured, lobbied, patrolled state-owned archaeological sites in the

George Luer records the damage to one of many sites eroding into Charlotte Harbor, May, 1988. (Photo by Bob Edic.)

area, and reported on any vandalism.

Meanwhile, I discovered I was involved with another cultural resource in danger of disappearing. A traditional way of life that had survived for more than six thousand years—Charlotte Harbor's fishing industry and its fisherfolk—were also in danger of extinction.

Like archaeological and historic sites, unwritten knowledge about local environments and their resources is also a non-renewable cultural resource. I realized that Charlotte Harbor's fishing traditions, like the Big Mound Key artifacts, were in danger of being lost if not collected and archived. I felt compelled to investigate the changes that were causing the demise of this tradition.

My interest was further inspired by Charles Dana Gibson's research on the settlement of the historic fishing communities of western Charlotte Harbor. His book, *Boca Grande: A Series of Historical Essays*, provided me with a valuable research tool for understanding Charlotte Harbor's fishing heritage (Gibson 1982).

With the traditional fisherfolk way of life changing rapidly, it became imperative that someone begin collecting oral histories with the oldest fisherfolk. The necessity for recording and archiving their stories was as apparent as the need for salvage archaeology on endangered sites.

With state permits, volunteer Edwin Woolverton, geologist Darden Hood, and archaeologist George Luer (left to right) profile a fire pit exposed in one of the bulldozer cuts on Big Mound Key, May, 1982. (Photo by Bob Edic.)

I had worked at the Boca Grande Fishery on Gasparilla Island from 1980 to 1984. As part of Charlotte Harbor's commercial fishing industry, I got to know people who were making a living from fishing there. I familiarized myself with the history of the region's fishing industry and sought to meet more people.

Tom Parkinson, my employer who had managed the Boca Grande Fishery for the past forty-five years, agreed to be my key informant. He introduced me to many of the senior fisherfolk whose heritage extends back to the late nineteenth- and early twentieth-century pioneer fishing communities of Cayo Costa, Coral Creek, Peacons Cove, Gasparilla Village, and Boca Grande.

Their life experiences are a direct connection to the past, and they are a valuable link to the historical fishing heritage of Charlotte Harbor. Their stories shed light on many aspects of Charlotte Harbor's fishing traditions. Some examples are the importance of certain marine species and when, where, and how they were caught; changes in the environment; and fishing methods. What we learn from them can be compared with

Tom Parkinson after his retirement. Tom and I had just returned from Useppa Island in 1989 where the Florida Museum of Natural History was conducting archaeological excavations. Tom had not visited the island since 1932. I recorded his reflections on the changing landscape. The loading dock of the Boca Grande Fishery and our apartment can be seen in the background. (Photo by Bob Edic.)

I first met Nellie Coleman on Pine Island in 1990 during our excavations at the Pineland site. Here she shows me many of the pictures she has saved from her early days on Cayo Costa. (Photo courtesy of J. C. Dewing.)

the archaeological records of previous fishing cultures, and remnants of past fishing practices can be identified. Some of these fishing practices probably were passed down from earlier fisherfolk, including the Calusa Indians and Spanish Cubans. What the fisherfolk say may help us to identify and understand prehistoric fishing practices and the fishing artifacts found in Charlotte Harbor's archaeological sites.

Fish Houses

The rich fishing grounds in the Charlotte Harbor area were destined to be the center of a booming industry. By 1900, the discovery of phosphate up the Peace River had brought the railroad to Punta Gorda. The railroad also opened the area to winter visitors, many of whom were sport fishermen. Many local fishermen supplemented their incomes as fishing guides after mullet season. Useppa and the outer islands became the center of this new industry.

In 1899, the Florida Fish and Ice Company opened for business at the rail head in Punta Gorda. Inexpensive transportation and ice for shipping "fresh fish" to northern markets were now in place. Soon after, Chadwick Brothers, the West Coast Fish Company, the Punta Gorda Fish Company, and others entered the market. Skilled fisherfolk were in high demand. This new lucrative business now required more people than were locally available to supply the expanding market for its products. Peacons Cove, a salt fishery that had been in operation since the 1870s, was assimilated by this new enterprise (Gibson 1982:57-58). This fate was typical of most of the area's salt fisheries.

Men were recruited from the Carolinas to join in. Many were brought down by rail in box cars specifically outfitted for the trip (Gibson 1982:56-57). Some were accompanied by their families, but most were single men looking for a chance to make money. Others came from throughout Florida. The fish companies initially supplied the boats and fishing equipment. Small fish-buying houses were set up in remote areas throughout Charlotte Harbor. Houseboats (called "lighters") and stilt houses were built over the water and managed by the fish companies. However, most of the fishermen just set up camp near the fish houses. A company "run boat" delivered ice and supplies for the fishermen and picked up the fish every couple of days.

Many fishing areas traditionally used by local fisherfolk were invaded by these new transient fishermen. Territorial confrontations were at times brutal. Areas such as Turtle Bay and Bull Bay near the Cape Haze Peninsula and Cayo Costa became legendary as places to be avoided. In a way, this served to limit the number of people fishing certain areas. Territoriality is a form of conservation as old as fishing itself.

A fish house built at the railroad stop on the north end of Gasparilla Island around 1914 supplied ice from the mainland, and the fish were packed and shipped north "fresh" by rail.

Sixteen small houses soon were built to attract not only fishermen, but also their families. The settlement was known as Gasparilla Village. It was comprised mostly of fisherfolk from Peacons Cove, Coral Creek, and the surrounding area. This was a more stable community complete with a school, a general store, and access to rail transportation. This broke the isolation for the fisherfolk and made it more compatible with family life.

The basic operation of the fish house changed little until quite recently. Its basic function was to buy fresh seafood products desired by the market and to resell them for a profit. The fish house still supplied the ice and provided a close reliable market for the catch. In return it got a reasonable assurance that the catch was sold exclusively to it for a fair market price. Fishermen remained loyal to the fish company, even when prices paid elsewhere were slightly higher. When other companies were not buying fish, the fish house would still buy or take small catches on consignment. This bond between the fisherfolk and the fish house was mutually beneficial.

In 1945 Walter Gault moved the fishing operations in Gasparilla Village to Placida. The land that he leased from the railroad was sold to Sunset Realty Company (H. L. Schwartz). It was named the Gasparilla Fishery. He built an ice plant to be self-sufficient. Probably because of his displeasure with the railroad company, he shipped fish overland by truck. Today the fishery is still owned and operated by his descendants.

The Gasparilla Fishery purchased a satellite fish house on

Gasparilla Village, circa 1920. Note net spreads and houses built by railroad in background. Note seine nets used for mackerel. The nets have been limed and hung to dry on net spreads. (Photo courtesy of Janice Busby.)

Gasparilla Island in 1939. Originally built by the Punta Gorda Fish Company in the early 1900s, it was located on the south end of the Gasparilla Inn golf course at the end of a long dock. The remains of the old pilings can still be seen out in the bay. Called the Boca Grande Fishery, it was managed by Tom Parkinson.

*Some of the
children pictured:
Albert Lowe
Gussie Cole
Bert Cole
Margaret Cole
Raymond Lowe
Oveda Rye
Audrey Rye
Van Bass
Genevieve
    Downing
Austin Bass
Ansell
    Underwood
Everton
    Underwood
Elsie Sands*

Gasparilla School, class of 1924. John Fish, teacher. (Photo courtesy of Eunice Albritton.)

Tom ran a run boat between Placida and the fish house until the Boca Grande Causeway was built in 1958. Before that, the island was reached only by rail and ferry service. Many of my informants say building the bridge was the biggest change to the island in their lifetimes. It brought easy access to the island and changed the community for the worse.

In 1980, the retail market where Tom had lived and raised his family was sold by the Fishery to raise money for inheritance taxes. The retail business was moved to the Boca Grande fish house. Tom built a

In 1941 a more protected spot was built in the Boca Grande Bayou (next to Sam Whidden's boat weights). A retail market in the center of town sold locally caught fish to the restaurants and the public. An apartment was provided upstairs for Tom and his family.

home on the island on a piece of property he bought from his son, Sam Parkinson. This left the apartment over the fish house open, an essential benefit for getting and keeping help.

Soon after, I was employed by the Boca Grande Fishery. My responsibilities were to ensure that a supply of ice was available, to pack the catch, and to haul the fish to Placida. Fishermen came and went at various times of the day and night, depending on the tides. Their boats needed to be iced before they went out fishing. When they returned, their catch was weighed and iced for shipping.

My family and I had moved to Boca Grande from upstate New York to avoid the brutal winters. While I enjoyed the mild winters in

Tom and daughter Carolyn Parkinson at Boca Grande Fishery, circa 1944. (Photo courtesy of Carolyn Parkinson Nabers.)

Florida, I still shoveled more ice than I ever had up north. My compensation was the apartment over the fish house, minimum wages with plenty of overtime, and all the mullet my family and I could eat. Not a bad deal considering everything — I was satisfied.

Tom came to the dock every day at sunset and sunrise to check on the whereabouts of fishermen. They were se-

cretive about their fishing locations, but Tom always knew
where they had gone and when
they were expected to return. In
effect, he provided a safety net for
the fishermen.

Although the fishermen always played up their distrust of
the fish buyers, they had a mutual
respect for Tom. Most had known
him all their lives. Because I
worked for Tom, I received similar
treatment. If a fisherman had a
large catch, he would bring it directly to Placida, saving us hours
of labor and valuable ice. During
off hours, the fishermen would ice
their boats and pack the fish themselves.

By the 1980s, territorial confrontations over fishing grounds
had taken a less violent form than

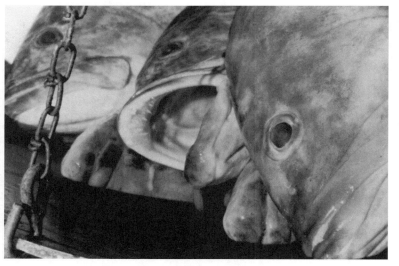

Fresh red grouper being weighed at fish house, Boca Grande. (Photo by Bob Edic.)

at the turn of the century. The
methods of intimidation were
now quite different. During the
"run season" in the Cape Haze
area, mullet would gather in
schools and run out to the Gulf of
Mexico to spawn. This activity
was triggered by cold fronts passing through the area in the fall.
The fishing boats would line up

off the Cape
waiting for their
turn to strike the
mullet school
with their nets.
There would be
more mullet than
any one person
could catch, but
not enough for
everyone. Many
fishermen would
endure the long line, camping for
several days to reserve their
places; others would not think it
worth their while and leave. Some
would take a smaller strike or go
elsewhere to fish. During large
runs, several boats in line would
go in jointly on a catch. Being able
to predict local weather patterns,
keeping abreast of the tides, and

predicting the daily movements of the fish enhanced the chances of a successful catch for the local fishermen.

I had the pleasure of going mullet fishing with some of the old timers, such as Louis and Alfonso Darna. While waiting for a strike, I observed their special skills. Their local knowledge of the harbor fascinated me. They would sing to the birds and talk to the fish, which would answer back. They had a reverence for the environment that I had never known. When the strike was successful, I helped clear the net and pack the fish. The money from the catch was divided evenly: one third for the captain, one third for the help, and one third for boat expenses. In a strange way I felt guilty taking my share. I never envisioned myself as a commercial fisherman. The work was hard and the hours long, but I learned a lot from my experiences.

Archaeologist George Luer was a frequent visitor to the Boca Grande fish house. We rummaged through the fish carcasses, collecting and measuring various bones for comparative analysis. He was excavating the fire pit exposed by the vandalism on Big Mound Key, finding it to be an invaluable resource. I am sure both Tom and the fishermen at first thought we were crazy, but they soon became interested in the previous fishing cultures that had inhabited the harbor. George gave me a tape recorder and encouraged me to collect information from the fishermen that was pertinent to our research.

Filleting fish for the growing retail business kept Tom busy for most of the day. More restaurants were opening, and more people were staying on the island every year. They all wanted fresh fish. I soon added filleting to my fishhouse skills.

Mary, Tom's wife, took care of the retail customers and kept the books on the entire operation. All monies and receipts went into a cigar box. It was tallied weekly and brought over to the Gasparilla Fishery at Placida every Friday. She spent a good deal of time at the Boca Grande fish house but was never officially on the payroll. Tom's salary as manager was slightly more than mine, but he

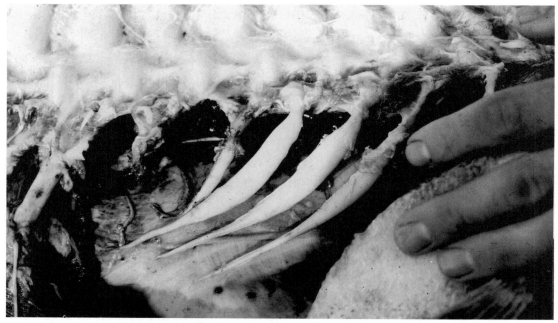

Exposed rib bones of a twelve-pound Crevalle Jack (Caranx hippos) *collected for comparative analysis at the Boca Grande Fishery, 1982. (Photo by George Luer.)*

sistible sum at the time. Some of the senior fishermen realized a retirement from the sale of their homes. As a result though, they were forced to move away from the community where they had lived all their lives. Housing, dockage, and a place to store equipment were now at a premium for many fisherfolk.

Tom was perturbed that fewer fish now came into the fish house from local fishermen and more varieties of non-local fish were shipped in from distant markets. He wanted to see the money remain in the local economy and was reluctant to change his way of doing business.

Many of the local people on the island had worked for Tom at

never received overtime for the long hours he put in. A bonus at Christmas usually compensated for any inequalities.

As the island's population increased during the 1980s, island property values became exorbitant. Many local fishermen who could not afford to rent on the island moved to the mainland. Huge increases in property taxes forced others to sell their property for what they considered an irre-

one time or another through the years. I found him very easy going, although the work was hard. He once told me, "You may not be the best worker I ever had, but you've worked for me longer than anyone else," but I found this hard to believe.

We had become close friends. He often joked about having only a sixth-grade education and having me, a college graduate, working for him. But I was learning much more from him than he would ever learn from me.

In 1984 I left the Boca Grande fish house to work full-time on the pressing archaeological needs in the harbor. The Gasparilla Fishery sent over Steve Lasher, a fisherman from Yankeetown, Florida, as my replacement. Tom continued to manage the business for several more years. The number of fishermen had dropped from more than fifty when I first started to fewer than ten. The Gasparilla Fishery eventually moved its fish-buying business to Placida but continued the retail market at the old fish house on Boca Grande.

Without his fishermen and their seafood products, Tom retired in 1986 after forty-six years.

Steve Lasher took over as manager.

The Boca Grande retail market was later moved to Placida, and the fish house sold, leaving the island without a fish house and the fresh local fish it provided.

I had the privilege of spending hundreds of hours "talking old times" with Tom and gleaned a view of the fishing heritage of which he was so much a part. It was Tom who inspired my interest in the oral history of the area's senior fisherfolk.

The run boat "Wallace" from Punta Gorda Fish Co.

that serviced Charlotte Harbor, picking up fish

and delivering ice and supplies, circa early 1930s.

(Photo courtesy of Richard Coleman.)

CHAPTER 2

Charlotte Harbor Fishing

Fishing

Fishing, as the term is used here, is not the romantic avocation espoused by Izaak Walton. Hook and line fishing is a small part of the technology on which past cultures in the Charlotte Harbor area have depended. Which species of fish or shellfish are gathered and how are matters of cultural preference. For example, fish can be netted, speared, trapped, clubbed, lassoed, poisoned, or hooked. Fishing also includes gathering shellfish as well as procuring other marine products, such as sea turtles. Throughout history, capture was usually accomplished in the most economical way possible to ensure a reliable catch for today and tomorrow.

Certain fish have to be targeted in specific ways to be caught. Many, like bay anchovies, are too small to be caught on hooks. Others, such as mullet, do not readily take a baited hook. Nets and spears then become invaluable tools. Some powerful predators—such as large shark, large snook, redfish, and trout—damage natural-fiber nets and have to be caught by other means, such as clubbing and hooking (Kozuch 1993:19). Crabs and shellfish living on the shallow grass flats and sand bars can be gathered easily on low tides. Accurate prediction of tidal episodes is the key to success. Food fish can even be gathered by hand very efficiently during some natural disasters, such as storms, winter freezes, or red tides.

The Charlotte Harbor Area

The Charlotte Harbor area is a naturally rich estuarine environment located in the mild subtropical climate of southwest Florida, stretching from Lemon Bay to Estero Bay. The region encompasses the coastal shoreline of the archaeological area called "Caloosahatchee" by Randolph Widmer (1988:79). For our purposes, the Charlotte Harbor area is divided into four major sections: Charlotte Harbor proper, Pine Island Sound, San Carlos Bay, and Estero Bay.

The Charlotte Harbor area is one of Florida's largest estuarine systems with over four hundred miles of shore line. Three major rivers—the Peace, the Myakka, and the Caloosahatchee—drain over two and one-half million acres of interior Florida. The health of the estuarine region is directly correlated with the contents of this drainage.

Charlotte Harbor's 225,000 acres of nutrient-rich water flows around Cape Haze Peninsula. Waters partially blocked by Gasparilla and Cayo Costa islands flow through Pine Island Sound and Matlacha Pass to join the Caloosahatchee River in San Carlos Bay. The estuarine region is fringed with red mangroves and dotted with many islands. Extensive seagrass beds are found in the shallow waters.

Salt marshes, mud flats, and oyster reefs are located in the tidal zone. The estuary is frequently inundated by strong high tides and provides ideal conditions for marine life to flourish. A series of barrier islands forms a buffer zone to protect it all from the Gulf of Mexico. Ever-changing passes separating the barrier islands control the mixture of salt and fresh water in the harbor.

Although the Charlotte Harbor area is said to be one of Florida's least environmentally impacted estuarine systems, Tables 1 and 2 show that its wetland areas have decreased by 23%, seagrass beds by 29%, salt marshes by 51%, mudflats by 76%, and oyster reefs by 39% between 1945 and 1982 (Haddad and Hoffman 1986:182). Now we realize that many marine species are on the decline in the Charlotte Harbor area, largely because of such significant habitat losses. Changes in water and sediment flow due to the construction of sea walls, causeways, and dredging of waterways and canals have had devastating results. Eutrophication—excessive plant growth in marine environments caused by an increase in nutrients—has upset the natural balance of the coastal estuaries. As a food-producing resource, the Charlotte Harbor area supplies 50% of Florida's west-coast commercial landings of redfish, trout, and mullet, but yields are declining.

As a result, the commercial fisherfolk's traditional way of life is also endangered. The sport-fishing

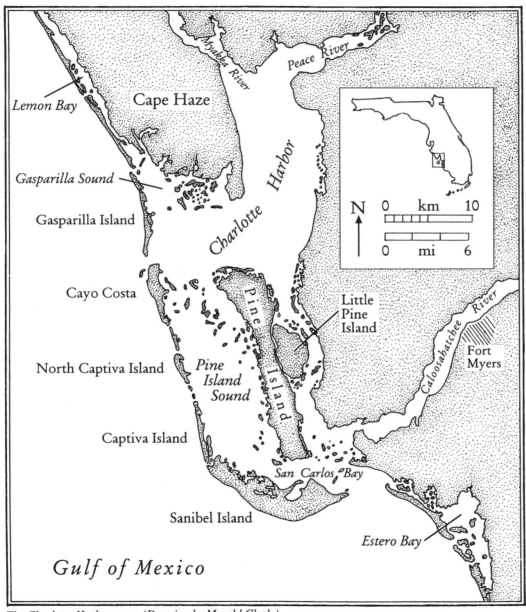

The Charlotte Harbor area. (Drawing by Merald Clark.)

industry, a more recent phenomenon, depends on many of the same resources for its livelihood. Modern fishing practices are rapidly changing as a result of the declining fish populations available to the commercial and sport fishing industries. Increasing regulation in response to "overfishing" is only a symptom of the real problem: loss of habitat. In most cases, new regulations hurt both the commercial and sport fishing industries. Economic considerations are now forcing many of the younger generation of commercial fisherfolk into other vocations.

Traditional fishing is a special knowledge passed down from generation to generation and it is only one generation away from being lost forever. Today's senior fisherfolk are the only remaining people to have fished without power boats and to have used natural-fiber nets, likely much the same way as their predecessors, the Spanish Cuban and Native American fisherfolk. They are witnesses to the fishing practices of yesterday and today. They can provide information about fishing that can be found no-where else to help us understand better the environmental and cul-tural changes that have occurred in this area.

The First Estuarine Description of Charlotte Harbor?

INSTRUCTIONS TO GO TO PENSACOLA, ON A ROUTE DIFFERING FROM THE FORMER

The Dry Tortugas lie in lat. 24°:25' and stretch northward as far as lat. 24°:45" N. The south end lies N 40°:W. 31 leagues from the Havana, or N ½ W 22 leagues from Bahia Honda, the direct course from the Tortugas to Pensacola is N 34° W, and the distance 142 leagues. But the fastest way is to run N ½ E 35 leagues, by which means you will make the land in lat. 26° 46' N; where is a large harbour called Charlotte harbour; here, in case of necessity, you may refresh, as it affords excellent water in many places, especially on a high island, whose north end is a broken bluff, and which shews itself very remarkable as soon as you are well shot in; there is likewise plenty of fish, and the islands are flocked with large herds of deer; there are 4 or 5 inlets into this bay; but the one that lies in the above latitude is deepest, it has 15 or 16 feet water on its bar; the southernmost is the next best, and it has 14 feet on its bar; this lies at lat. 26 ° 30, and is remarkable for the coast taking a sudden turn from N NW, to directly west, only for about 9 or 10 miles; when it again resumes its former direction; this nook in the land, forms what the Spaniards call Ensenada de Carlos, i.e., Charles's Bay, the piece of coast that trends E and W, is the beach of an island called Sanybel, this place is further remarkable for a great number of pine-trees without tops standing at the bottom of the bay, there is no place like to it, in the whole extent of this coast; the northernmost entrance is likewise remarkable for a singular hammock of pine-trees, or a grove standing very near the beach, than which there is none like it anywhere hereabouts;

Bernard Romans
1775

Table 1. Historical and Recent Acreages of Land Use and Vegetation Categories in Charlotte Harbor (Source: Haddad and Hoffman 1986:182).

Land Use or Vegetation Category	Acreage		
	1945	1982	% Change
Urban	3,710	96,105	+ 2490
Agriculture	13,137	10,283	- 22
Rangeland	106,219	20,704	- 81
Forestland	34,583	40,491	+ 17
Water	288,799	312,705	+ 8
Wetlands	160,226	123,903	- 23
Barrenland	6,202	7,826	+ 26
Transportation and Utilities	1,801	3,433	+ 91

Table 2. Historical and Recent Acreages of Marine Wetland Habitats (Source: Haddad and Hoffman 1986:182).

Wetland Habitat	Acreage		
	1945	1982	% Change
Seagrasses	82,959	58,495	- 29
Mangroves	51,524	56,631	+ 10
Saltmarsh	7,251	3,547	- 51
Mudflats	11,206	2,723	- 76
Oyster Reefs	806	488	- 39

Thomas Lowe, Sr., with daughter Ella
and son Albert in a pole skiff at
Gasparilla Village, circa 1920.
(Photo courtesy of Janice Busby.)

CHAPTER 3

Six Thousand Years of Tradition

Hundreds of archaeological sites, representing Native American and European-American fishing cultures, are located in the Charlotte Harbor area. These sites, which span a successful occupation of over six thousand years, are the remnants of cultures that took advantage of the bountiful marine menu through time.

In southwest Florida, fishing has long supplied protein to growing human populations. The earliest date for occupation in the Charlotte Harbor area is about 13,500 years ago, based on evidence recovered from Little Salt Spring near North Port (Clausen et al. 1979). Artifacts found there suggest a hunting and gathering way of life for a nomadic group of people known as the Paleo Indians.

Paleo-Indian People

(11500-6500 B.C.)

The Paleo Indians were the earliest known people who came to the Florida peninsula more than thirteen thousand years ago. Florida's first "pioneers" were nomadic hunters and gatherers traveling in family bands in search of mastodon, bison, and other large game. About nine thousand years ago, as the climate gradually warmed, most Ice Age megafauna became extinct (possibly from human exploitation), and the people adopted new ways of survival. It is easy to speculate that Paleo people also harvested the rich bounty of the estuarine and coastal areas, then located two hundred miles to the west. Unfortunately, any early evidence for such coastal occupation has been drowned by rising sea levels.

Pre-Ceramic Archaic People

(6500-2000 B.C.)

The Archaic People were Florida's first "settlers." By eight thousand years ago, people had become less nomadic, and their populations had increased. They relied more on small-game hunting, gathering, and exploiting coastal marine resources. These were Charlotte Harbor's first settled residents.

Recent archaeological excavations on Horr's Island (in the Marco Island area, Collier County) and on Useppa Island (Lee County) provide clues to human activity during this period. Fishing artifacts and massive quantities of marine refuse indicate that Native Americans lived a more sedentary

Deer bones were used to make compound fish hooks, throat gorges, harpoon points, and other tools. Scale: ½ actual size. (Photo courtesy of FLMNH.)

Large fossil shark's tooth (notched)— found on Calusa Island. (Photo by Bob Edic.)

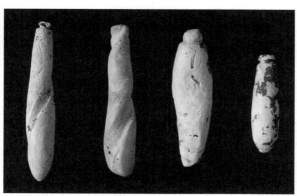

Possible fishing sinkers made from whelk and conch shells. Scale: ½ actual size. (Photo courtesy of FLMNH.)

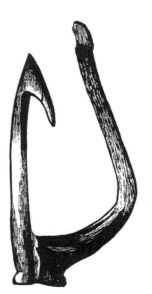

Composite fishhook made of carved bone, wood, and twine. (Drawing by Merald Clark.)

Ark shell net weights. Scale: ½ actual size. (Photo courtesy of FLMNH.)

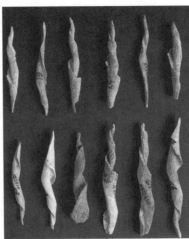

Lightning whelk throat gorges may have been used like fish hooks. I have caught fish using replicas of these. Scale: ½ actual size. (Photo courtesy of FLMNH.)

Chert knife blades found at Pineland are essential prehistoric fishing equipment. Scale: ½ actual size. (Photo courtesy of FLMNH.)

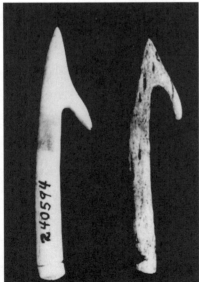

Carved bone barbs from composite fishhooks (see opposite page). Large fish were caught with such fishhooks. (Photo courtesy of FLMNH.)

Dugout canoe— Calusa family car. (Photo courtesy of FLMNH.)

life than previously thought. New radiocarbon dates demonstrate that this estuarine-based fishing culture was thriving almost six thousand years ago (Marquardt 1995; Russo 1991).

People of the Ceramic Period

(2000 B.C. – A.D. 500)

People of the Ceramic Period were "villagers" who lived on many of the shell mounds in the harbor, perhaps year around. Fragments of pottery bowls found on Calusa Island and in the Turtle Bay area indicate that people in this region began making crude, fiber-tempered ceramics about four thousand years ago. This pottery is some of the oldest found in North America. Quantities of later ceramics found at some local sites suggest that people were more sedentary. Because pottery is fragile and often heavy, it was not used extensively by nomadic cultures.

Calusa People

(A.D. 500 – 1750)

The people later known as the "Calusa" began to develop more complex social structures. Around A.D. 500 large shell mounds began to be constructed along the estuaries, some later incorporating courts and canals. Increasingly elaborate systems of trade began to appear. One indication is the wide diversity of ceramic debris found on such large sites as Big Mound Key and Pineland.

Spanish documents dating to the sixteenth century reveal that the Calusa had developed a complex cultural, economic, and political system. They had permanent villages, a vast trade network and transportation system, and a well-developed military. This was based on the natural abundance of the marine environment, not on agriculture (Hann 1991; Marquardt 1988:161-169; Marquardt 1992a). The rich coastal environment of southwest Florida filled the role usually played by agriculture in other complex societies (Goggin and Sturtevant 1964:207).

The Calusa dominated all of southwest Florida from Charlotte Harbor to the Keys at the time of first European contact in 1513. However, the sophisticated estuarine-based cultural system that flourished at Spanish contact vanished over the next two hundred years (Hann 1991:325-431; Marquardt 1988:176-185). Now all that remains are the archaeological record, brief mention in historic chronicles, and possibly some fishing practices still being used by contemporary fisherfolk.

For the Calusa, fishing was not just an economic endeavor—it was the mainstay of their lives. The very existence of the powerful Calusa kingdom and all who paid it tribute depended in large part on fishing. As fisherfolk, their lives were no doubt organized around the rich marine environment. Their religion, art, and social institutions depended on successful harvesting of the marine environment, an environment that they must have revered. The legacy of their maritime heritage is obvious from the marine refuse that comprises the mounds—the foundations of their major villages. No doubt, they also found and recognized the artifacts of their predecessors on the sites and realized the extensive duration of this maritime culture.

Charlotte Harbor's indigenous people lived with the estuarine environment continuously for six thousand years. Zoological and botanical data recovered from archaeological excavations at local precolumbian sites provide clues to this lengthy occupation. Procuring fish as their major source of protein (Walker 1992:356-357), these native people conserved their food resources by taking advantage of the diversity of species available. Black mangrove wood used as fuel for cooking and warmth was coppiced (trimmed) without killing the plant, showing a form of energy management (Scarry and Newsom 1992:389). The mounds themselves are perfect examples of solid waste management. The Calusa were not consummate conservationists, but they were not ignorant about their place in the environment. They had a special knowledge acquired over thousands of years, as well as the technology, social organization, and rituals necessary to create a surplus economy.

From the archaeological data recovered so far, we can now say with some certainty that the Calusa did not pass into oblivion as a result of overpopulation or by depletion of their fishing resources. Franciscan records show the Calusa were still in their homelands and still exerting pressure on other local groups as late as 1698 (Hann 1991). This was long after many other native Florida Indians had been missionized or dominated by European militarism. In any case, by 1711 the once powerful Calusa had been overrun by Creek and Yamassee Indians from the north. Many Calusa were sold into slavery; others fled into the Everglades and Florida Keys (Parks 1985:52-55). The Spanish attempted to rescue some of the remaining Calusa from the Keys and transport them to Cuba, but most died of diseases enroute (Hann 1991:325-333). The last sustained contact with remnant groups of Calusa was in 1743 in the Keys by Jesuits (Hann 1991:333). The marine wealth that was so much a part of their sustenance remained intact for the use of other peoples.

Historic Native American Groups

In the late 1600s, Indian refugees from colonial expansion in northern Florida and Georgia began to arrive in the Charlotte Harbor area (Swanton 1922:104). North Florida mission Indians fleeing the raids of the English Colonel James Moore may have settled in the area after 1704. Leon-Jefferson pottery from north Florida, typical of this time period, has been found on several sites in Charlotte Harbor, sites possibly abandoned by the original inhabitants and used by these new arrivals (Bullen and Bullen 1956).

The word "Indian" from this point on in history implies a mixture of various aboriginal groups. Among them were remnants of the once mighty Calusa nation. Spanish rule of the Caribbean and Florida resulted in a breakdown of the Calusa culture by the early 1700s. Scattered groups of mixed-blood natives living a nomadic existence were left. No doubt some of the Calusa bloodlines and fishing traditions were now dispersed among all groups that had moved into or passed through the Charlotte Harbor area.

This new mixture of Native Americans presented little threat to the Spanish Cubans. At first the Indians were allowed only restricted access to trade goods; no firearms, knives, other weapons, or metal objects could be legally traded (Dickinson 1985). As trading between Cubans and the Calusa continued, more and more European trade goods were desired. Knives and other metal objects (much sought-after trade items) became common, producing a lucrative business for both groups. The Indians traveled from Key West to Cuba by canoe, sometimes in as little as twenty four hours (Kerrigan 1951:344-345). They carried shark liver oil and ambergris (a secretion from whales used to make perfume), which were valuable commodities in the international market. Certain tree bark, fruit, hides, furs, live birds, and many other items were also traded (Covington 1959:116-117). West Indies monk seals and manatees, then common, were rendered for their fat to grease the bottoms of Spanish ships (Williams 1753:19).

The Spanish market for ambergris and other expensive goods created conditions favorable to a lucrative smuggling trade. Many Spanish ships plied the waters trading the fabric, metal tools, lead sinkers, fish hooks, nets, and boats much desired by the Indians. Tobacco, rum, coffee, sugar, arms, and ammunition soon entered the trading circle. The Calusa's passion for alcohol was well documented by the Spanish Jesuits (Hann 1991:326). Alcoholism that plagued Florida's native population was the result of contact with the Spanish and the introduction of their forms of alcoholic drinks. Before contact, the Indians had no interest in alcohol. But by the 1740s, "They neither wanted to become Christians or work for Cuban fishermen without it" (Hann 1991:326).

Spanish Cubans

By the beginning of the 1700s, the shallow fishing grounds around Cuba and the nearby islands were being depleted of their edible marine resources (Covington 1959:114). These areas had been used to supply protein to the vast Spanish enterprise in the New World for two hundred years. Despite the hostilities at first contact, trade between Cuba and the Indians of Charlotte Harbor was inevitable. The rich estuaries and coastal fishing grounds of southwest Florida were a close source of protein: mullet, redfish, pompano, grouper, sea turtles, and other marine products could be cured and easily shipped.

The Spanish quickly discovered the real treasure of Charlotte Harbor. Once the domain of the powerful Calusa, this prodigious breeding ground for fish was now open territory. Without the Calusa's highly organized exploitation of the area's marine resources, we can only imagine how prolific the environment must have been.

The Spanish at first did not know how to exploit the estuaries as the Calusa had done. Their fishing was mainly with hook and line in the shallow waters of the Gulf. Grouper were kept alive in the wells of their boats for return to Cuba. They also traded for cured mullet and mullet roe, conchs, and other commodities which the local Indians' knowledge of the estuaries produced (Gibson 1982:16). Cuban fishermen incorporated the Indians and their technology to exploit the fishing resource at first. "Silk grass" (the native bayonet plant, *Yucca aloifolia*) was used to make fiber for nets and cordage (Austin 1980:28). They built racks and hung fish to cure in the sun by air-drying (Covington 1959:118). Roe was soaked in salt water, then dried and pressed for shipping to Cuba.

When, where, and how to fish the estuaries was a special knowledge passed down from the Calusa and now in possession of the local Native American population.

The Spanish soon introduced more effective methods of procuring marine goods for the Cuban markets. The Spanish brought their own fishing technology: metal hooks, boats, large nets, salt for curing, and wooden barrels for shipping. The method of pressing, drying, and lightly salting mullet for shipment would soon change (Covington 1959:118). Cultural assimilation was increasing the variety of marine products.

Fish "ranchos" (fisheries) were set up and run by Spanish Cubans. The local Indians were hired to harvest and cure fish and other commodities for markets in Cuba (Gibson 1982:16). This new market resource was important to Cubans, because it gave them independence from "Yankee Cod," which was shipped from New England and the Canadian maritime colonies; and they preferred the fish from Florida (Forbes 1821:118; Gibson 1982:70). Cuba soon took over the fishing industry in the Charlotte Harbor area.

Spanish Indians

By the mid-1700s the Indians in Charlotte Harbor who fished for the Spanish had become known as "Spanish Indians." Although by now the Calusa, for the most part, had disappeared as a culture, it is possible that remnant groups of Calusa were still living in isolated areas of Charlotte Harbor. Creek and other Native American groups who were now entering the area did not have the same command as the Calusa did of how to exploit the local marine resources. Therefore, the Calusa's fishing skills would have been greatly desired by newly arriving Indian and Spanish fishermen alike. The Calusa could easily have assimilated with the Creeks and together joined the emerging fish ranchos now being set up in the area by the Spanish. According to James Covington (1959:118), many pure-blood Indians worked aboard the fishing vessels and were said to be "capable sailors." He also states that many of the "Spanish Indians" did not return seasonally with the Spanish to Cuba, but "remained and grew corn, peas and melons" (Covington 1959:118-120). This trait was more characteristic of the Creeks than the Calusa, who did not practice agriculture.

Many Cuban fishermen who settled in the area year around cohabited with or married Indian women, since it was not their custom to bring their spouses with them. Some of the marriages were recognized in Cuba, and children were sent to Cuba to be baptized and educated. Some stayed, secured jobs, and became Spanish subjects with full rights of citizenship (Covington 1959:119). By the early 1800s many "mixed blood Indians" had taken Spanish surnames. These became known as "Spanish Indians" to separate them from the local Native Americans (Gibson 1982:79; Neill 1955).

When the English took over Florida from the Spanish in 1763 at the end of the French and Indian War, Cuban fishing operations went on as usual for awhile. John Stuart, a British Indian agent, classified the renegades of the Creek Nation to the north as "cimmarones" (later "Seminoles") or "wild ones." The Creeks and other Indians were pushing farther and farther down the Florida peninsula, trying to escape the English to the north. They were viewed as a threat to English sovereignty. The English concluded there were no indigenous Native Americans left in Florida. This allowed all Indians to be labeled as Seminoles. Spanish trade with the Seminoles became illegal and was now considered smuggling. This disrupted Spanish fishing operations, and many fishermen returned to Cuba.

Spanish Indians from the fishing communities were allowed by the English to return to Cuba. Some 380 were shipped from Key West to Cuba in 1763 (Gibson 1982:14). Of course, not all the local people left the area. Many probably stayed at their isolated locations, unaffected by the English. Others went into hiding, surviving among the mangrove islands they knew so well (Gibson 1982:16).

England returned Florida to Spain in 1783 at the end of the American Revolution. Spain again legitimized trade between the Seminoles and the Cubans. Cuban fishermen and Spanish Indians who had left the area during English rule soon returned. Native Americans reappeared and were again employed by the Cuban fishing industry (Gibson 1982:17). This time the Cubans incorporated an even more effective method of curing fish. They packed fish in salt for a longer storage life than dried fish. Salt that could only be gotten legally from the king's warehouse in Havana soon became an expensive commodity on which a high tariff had to be paid. Fishermen were not allowed to make their own salt from sea water, and the Indians became even more dependent on the Spanish.

One use for this salt fish in Cuba was to feed the black slaves for whom Spain had developed a colonial market. Salt fish could be easily stored, transported, and used without fear of spoiling (Covington 1959:118).

An account by George Gauld, a British explorer who visited Charlotte Harbor in 1765, describes Spanish fish processing:

....They begin by pressing the fish with great weights (to remove the excess fluids and hasten drying time, which at the same time reduces maggot damage). Then it is split, salted, and hung to dry. The last operation is to pile it up in huts ready for loading. They supply Havana and the West Indies in Lent season. (Gauld 1790:13)

In the 1770s, Bernard Romans explored the Charlotte Harbor area. He stated that in a period of three years, one thousand tons of dried mullet were shipped to Havana from Charlotte Harbor. He also noted that Indians were still being used on most of the fish ranchos. In the winter months more than four hundred people were employed by the Cuban fisheries (Romans 1775:185).

José Caldez was the head ranchero for Spanish fishing operations in the Charlotte Harbor area from 1784 to 1836. He managed the various fishing operations from his headquarters on present-day Useppa Island (then called "Toampa," but soon changed to "Caldez Island"). His village was built on the west side of the island,

consisting of about twenty palmetto houses and a couple of schooners to run fish to Cuba (Gibson 1982:17-18). Three other fishing communities were located nearby under his command. Besides fishing, these people gardened and grew limes, oranges, and coconuts, which they traded to other fishermen (Williams 1837:25).

When the United States purchased Florida from Spain in 1821, the trading of Cuban goods (guns, ammunition, and rum) to the Seminoles became of interest to federal troops. A customs agent in the area at that time described the local Cuban fishermen "as being of the roughest types, many of whom were refugees from Spanish law" (Gibson 1982:17). Again, trading with the Indians was outlawed.

A group of runaway black slaves fleeing their masters in Georgia settled on Pine Island. They cut timber, fished, and traded with the Spanish. In return, they were given protection by the Spanish (Covington 1959:121). These runaway slaves also attracted U.S. government attention.

In Charlotte Harbor in 1824, U.S. Army Captain Isaac Clark met the Seminole Chief Jumper on Useppa Island (Gibson 1982:19). He was waiting for the return of his crew from Cuba with a supply of rum. Chief Jumper informed Captain Clark that trade between the Seminoles and Cuba had gone on since at least 1773, suggesting an earlier relationship between some of the Creek Indians from the north and the Spanish Indians in Charlotte Harbor (Covington 1959:117).

Dr. Henry Crews, a U.S. customs agent, was sent to Charlotte Harbor in 1832 to keep an eye on the situation. Crews and his family took up residence on Useppa Island where Caldez, now ninety years old, was still in charge of Cuban operations in the area. Crews could find out little about smuggling operations on Useppa and Cayo Pelau (also written as "Pelow" or "Pelew"), but he suspected Caldez was the ringleader (Gibson 1982:18; Neill 1955:45).

In 1835 a group of Seminoles ambushed and killed 105 of 108 soldiers under the command of Major Francis Dade north of Tampa. After the massacre, some of the Seminoles were forced south by federal reprisals. A band of twenty five Seminole braves, led by Chief Wyhokee fleeing through Charlotte Harbor, attacked and burned the settlement on Useppa Island. Dr. Crews' mutilated body was found along with a companion on an island not far away. José Caldez and many other members of his fishing operation returned to Cuba in their sailing sloop; others had to be rescued by federal troops (Gibson 1982:26-27). Spanish Indians either returned to Cuba with the Spanish or went into hiding with other Native American groups in the area.

The U.S. government initiated a federal Indian removal policy—a concept as insensitive as its name implies. Anyone even remotely Indian or Indian-like was to be

Palm thatch hut on central Cayo Costa, circa 1900. (Photo courtesy of Richard Coleman.)

José Gaspar the Pirate

José Gaspar is a fictitious pirate whom local legend claims ruled the southwest coast of Florida from 1783 to 1821. According to the myth, he maintained hideouts on Gasparilla Island and Cayo Pelau. He was not mentioned by any of the local fisherfolk or referred to by any early visitors to the area. No archaeological or historical documentation has been recovered to prove he ever existed.

Instead, historians theorize that Gasparilla Island and Pass were named for Friar Gaspar, based on maps predating the spurious pirate (Blunt and Bullen 1833). The persistence of the pirate legend and its mythical buried treasure has resulted in irreparable damage to many archaeological sites. The physical destruction by treasure hunters has marred the archaeological record forever.

rounded up and sent to Tampa Bay to await shipment to reservations in Oklahoma. Seven Cubans caught up in these raids were finally freed only after many protests (Grant 1953:365). By one account, a fisherman said that he had lost three wives to the federal Indian removal policy (Covington 1959:128). Due to Seminole attacks and U.S. troops in the area, the Cuban fishing operations and their communities on the outer islands were abandoned once again.

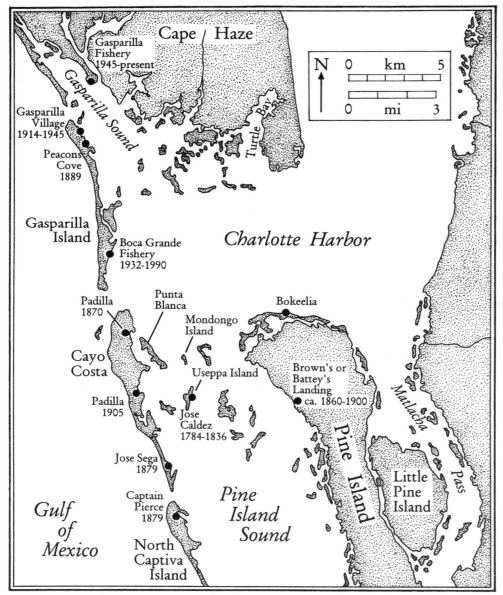

Map of fishing operations. (Drawing by Merald Clark.)

After 1845 when Florida became the twenty-seventh state, fishing communities again sprang up on Useppa (then called "Guiseppe"), northern Cayo Costa (at Burroughs Ranch), Mondongo, Punta Blanca, and Pineland (then called "Brown's"). Vegetable farms and citrus groves were started around Charlotte Harbor, many located on former Indian sites because of good drainage and the nutrients necessary for successful production. People in these communities had to swear allegiance to the United States (Gibson 1982:29-30).

Pursuing new American interests, U.S. Army Captain John Charles Casey was appointed Indian Commissioner for the removal of Seminoles from the area in 1849. Captain Casey had previous experience with the Indians and fishermen while at Fort Brooke in Tampa. Casey was said to be on good terms with the Indians and had previously negotiated with them. After Fort Brooke was severely damaged by a hurricane, Casey helped select a site for a new military outpost in Charlotte Harbor and assisted in the first U.S. Coast and Geodetic Survey of the area. In 1850 Fort Casey was established on Useppa Island to protect settlers (Matthews 1983:201-202). The settlement appears to have been short-lived, since an 1859 survey shows Useppa as being overgrown. The location of the "old wharf" and four small buildings at the site of the present-day Useppa Island clubhouse are indicated as well as a dock on the eastern side of the is-

land. The location of the fort has not been confirmed (Gibson 1982:31).

From 1861 to 1865, the Civil War introduced a different set of variables in Charlotte Harbor. A Union encampment was set up on Useppa Island in 1861 and a blockade of Charlotte Harbor was in place until 1865, effectively curtailing most of the fishing and smuggling operations. Some of the settlements may have remained throughout the war, providing fresh fish, fruit, and vegetables for Union troops (Gibson 1982:41).

After the war, Cubans returned and fish ranchos once again were established in Charlotte Harbor (U.S. Census 1870). This time they brought their own crews from Cuba. Some might have been descendants of Spanish Indians who

had fled to Cuba after the Seminole raid and Indian removal policy. These people possibly carried the last vestiges of the Calusa bloodlines and were possibly the last to possess directly the oral traditions of Charlotte Harbor's original inhabitants. Soon they would be known as "Americans."

George Goode conducted a survey in the 1870s for the U.S. Commission of Fish and Fisheries. He described some of the fishing operations in Charlotte Harbor:

The Captiva fish ranch run by a Captain Pierce and thirty "Conchs" [a term for people from Key West] produced 660,000 pounds of salted mullet and 49,500 pounds of dried mullet roe. On south Cayo Costa, Jose Sega, the head ranchero along with 26 fishermen, yielded about a quarter of that amount. Ranchero Tariva Padilla (Captain "Pappy") and his crew of 23 Spanish and one American produced about the same. One on Gasparilla Island's northern end was run by Captain Beacon and 30 "Conchs." It produced 550,000 pounds of mullet and 44,000 pounds of roe. (Goode 1844-1887:13)

Beacon's operation (located at Peacons Cove) was more permanent and its products were superior to those of the Spanish fisheries. The mullet and their roe from these fisheries were salted, processed, and shipped to Cuba. Prices in the 1870s were four cents a pound for salted mullet and five cents a pound for the cured mullet roe (Goode 1844-1887:13).

The following excerpt from the Goode Report describes the fishing resources of Charlotte Harbor at that time:

....Being in immense schools, the upper portion of the bay (harbor) affords inexhaustible feeding grounds, which are exceptionally free of pre-dacious fish. When leaping from the water in great abundance, the mullet make noises like the sound of thunder; this continues day and night. (Goode 1844-1887:14)

In 1894 Chicago streetcar magnate John M. Roach bought Useppa Island and built the original Tarpon Inn on the northern end of the island. Useppa became the center of tarpon fishing in the Charlotte Harbor area, attracting many of Roach's friends and business associates during the winter months. The visitors employed guides who had their roots in the area's rich fishing traditions. Tarpon and many other kinds of fish were caught.

After the turn of the century, many Cuban fishing boats, called "smacks," were again plying the coastal waters of southwest Florida in search of grouper. The shallow grouper fishing grounds off the Bahamian Banks, Cayo Sals, and the Dry Tortugas were depleted from overfishing. Southwest Florida was now the closest source for grouper that could be caught in shallow waters (under fifty feet) with hand lines.

Grouper caught in deeper water did not acclimate to the "live wells" the Spanish used to transport their catch back to Cuba (Gibson 1982:58). Live bottom zones—rocky bottoms that attract marine life—located just twenty miles off the southwest Florida coast were not being used extensively by local fisherfolk and were made to order for Cuba's grouper fleet. The Cuban grouper smacks used hand lines and mullet for bait. The Cuban fishermen could readily obtain salted mullet and other local commodities for their return to Cuba by trading rum (*aguardiente*) and cigars. Judging from the number of demi-john bottles (rum bottles) found in the area dating to this time and earlier, the long tradition of smuggling was still alive and well.

A raid by the U.S. Revenue Service in 1901 led to the arrest and conviction of head ranchero Tariva Padilla of Cayo Costa for smuggling. Padilla and his associates were accused of supplying entertainment contraband to the fishing communities and sport fishing industry in the area. Large quantities of rum, cigars, and tobacco as well as their sailing boats were confiscated (*Punta Gorda Herald*, Jan. 24, 1902).

The Padillas were labeled as "squatters," their homestead was burned, and they were banished from northern Cayo Costa, which had been a military reservation since 1848. A few years later they returned to central Cayo Costa and Punta Blanca, just to the south of the military reservation. They continued fishing and trading with Cuba (Gibson 1982:54). Tariva died in 1910 and was buried in the old cemetery on the north end of Cayo Costa.

The smuggling of Cuban rum boomed during prohibition. Testimony from oral history informants indicates that the wealthy winter residents of the area preferred rum to the local bootleg whiskey (moonshine) with its devastating effects. Smuggling evidently continued long after the Pilotage Act was supposed to have ended it in the 1930s.

Twentieth-Century Fisherfolk

Soon after the turn of the century, "fish ice" changed the fishing industry. In 1905-1907, a rail spur was built by the Charlotte Harbor and Northern Railroad for transporting phosphate to the newly built Port Boca Grande (Williams and Cleveland 1993:177-178). In 1914, a fish house was built by the railroad on the northern end of Gasparilla Island and leased. Ice was brought in to what would grow to become Gasparilla Village and fish were packed out by rail.

During World War II, commercial fishing was considered essential to the war effort, and many fishermen were exempted from active duty. Mullet fishing continued, but higher prices for grouper and the availability of guide boats from the now inactive sport-fishing fleet favored the development of the grouper fishing industry. Boca Grande Pass at first was very productive, but fishing pressure soon forced the grouper boats farther offshore. The closest live-bottom zone offshore was the same area used earlier by the Cuban grouper "smacks." These areas had not been intensively fished for over a decade (Gibson 1982:67).

This area provided local fishermen with an important economic resource until a severe red tide wiped out the grouper industry in 1947. Although records show red tides occurring in the Charlotte Harbor area in 1946, 1947, and 1948, the red tide of 1947 was one of the earliest and worst in the memory of local fisherfolk.

The gulf shrimping industry began trawling the soft sandy bottoms along the southwest Florida coast around 1949 (Gibson 1982: 76). Bait shrimpers soon began trawling the shallow grass flats in the estuaries to supply the growing recreational market.

By the 1960s, run boats from Punta Gorda Fish Company no longer picked up fish from the outer islands. Many commercial fishermen fished only during peak seasons, supplementing their incomes with other types of work during slack periods. As the sport-fishing industry and related business grew, many commercial fisherfolk became seasonal fishing guides.

In the 1980s an insatiable Japanese demand drove wholesale prices for mullet roe to over $12 per pound. These prices attracted many outsiders to the Charlotte Harbor fishery during the spawning season (November to January). They targeted the spawning female mullet roe, called "red roe." By the mid-1990s the price of "red mullet roe" had increased eight-fold. Overfishing was the result.

In 1991 the Florida Conservation Association (FCA) and *Florida*

The railroad entering Gasparilla Village looking south toward Boca Grande, circa 1920. The fish house is on the left side of the tracks and the IGA store owned by Gus Cole is on the right. (Photo courtesy of Richard Coleman.)

Twentieth-century fisherfolk have seen many changes: the first motorized fishing boats in the area around 1910, pole skiffs, sailing boats, row boats, mullet boats (locally called "kicker boats"), and luxurious sport fishing boats. They were the last to use natural-fiber nets of cotton and flax, replaced by nylon and monofilament nets. They witnessed the changes in fishing techniques from stop-netting to electronic fish finders and aerial surveillance of fish migration. These innovations in fishing technology have led to the demise of the premodern fishing traditions.

The days of an unregulated fishing industry are long past. *Sportsman* magazine began lobbying for an amendment to the Florida Constitution to ban the use of gill and entanglement nets in Florida's inshore waters. In 1994 Florida voters approved the amendment by a three-to-one margin. The law (which took effect in July, 1995) will severely affect the livelihood of Charlotte Harbor's fisherfolk. The Organized Fishermen of Florida (OFF) and the Southeastern Fisheries Association are currently fighting the amendment in state and federal courts. The outcome is uncertain.

Cayo Costa fisherman Alfonso Darna, at Punta Blanca fish house in his boat "Skip Jack," with 6500 pounds of mullet that still need to be cleared from the net. They were caught in Captiva Pass, circa 1938. The man to the right on the dock is Joe DeWitt, known to most as "Chief." (Photo courtesy of Nellie Coleman.)

Walter Gault. (Photo courtesy of Eunice Albritton.)

Walter Gault built a fleet of shrimp boats in 1950s. (Photo by Bob Edic.)

Improvements in fishing technology, more people exploiting the resources for both commercial and recreational purposes, and loss of habitat have severely limited catches. Sport fishing has become the rival of commercial fishing, each industry blaming the other for its shortcomings. Both are dependent on a marine environment that is losing its habitat rapidly because of booming development. The effects of the constitutional amendment banning net fishing have devastated the commercial fishing industry. In the short run, political and financial power are on the side of the sport-fishing industry, and the traditional commercial fisherfolk could disappear by the twenty-first century. However, no one will win in the long run if the source of the problem—improper human manipulation of the estuarine system—is not corrected before it is too late. Through proper management, the marine resource could again provide a bountiful existence for all.

In Charlotte Harbor today, many sport-fishing guides and commercial fishermen can trace their ancestry to the pioneer fish ranchos. Traditional fishing techniques—when, where, and how to fish—were passed down to these fourth- and fifth-generation fisherfolk, the last keepers of a fishing heritage. Their history is a direct connection to the past and a valuable link to the centuries-old fishing traditions of Charlotte Harbor.

Charles "Pork Chops" Futch, Jr. with cast net, Gasparilla Village, circa 1930. (Photo courtesy of Eunice Albritton.)

CHAPTER 4

Fisherfolk

The fisherfolk of Charlotte Harbor are part of the fishing continuum passed down from the Calusa Indians and their predecessors through the Spanish Indians to the Cuban fishermen. This heritage, still present today in the memories of the last people who lived it—the senior fishing community of Charlotte Harbor—is one generation away from oblivion. Conversations with senior fisherfolk enable us to see through the eyes of the last generation of people who practiced early twentieth-century fishing. Some of their traditions—such as natural-fiber nets, hand-powered and sailing boats, tides and weather observations—have their roots in prehistory. Collecting and archiving their recollections will allow future researchers to evaluate what they learn along with current and future archaeological data recovered from the Harbor. Preserving what they know will increase our understanding of the different fishing cultures that inhabited Charlotte Harbor before our time.

The Charlotte Harbor fisherfolk introduced here shed light on premodern fishing techniques. They discuss their life experiences on subjects of archaeological interest—the lifeways of different cultures that occupied this area through time. How they lived, fished, and dealt with natural forces gives us a direct connection to the past.

Interview Techniques

I identified potential informants by compiling kinship charts to locate older individuals with hereditary ties to the pioneer fishing communities. Ten who were formally interviewed have fished in the Charlotte Harbor area all their lives and are the basis for this book. Many other fisherfolk were also consulted.

I used a questionnaire in audiotaped interviews that could be transcribed to recover comparative information on fishing practices and environmental changes.

A release form was presented to each informant so that all data collected could be archived and reproduced. At times, getting the form signed was difficult, because many elder fisherfolk do not like signing anything.

Ten taped interviews were collected and archived. The interviews were transcribed by the Oral History Department and sent back to the informant for corrections. The corrected transcripts are archived at the George Smathers Library, Special Collections, University of Florida. A copy of each archived transcript was sent to the informant or his/her family.

Thomas S. "Tommy" Parkinson

(Photo, 1985, courtesy of Boca Beacon.*)*

Tom Parkinson was my key informant and reviewed other informants' transcripts for me. Tom was born in the town of Charlotte Harbor in 1914. He was formerly a commercial fisherman (1924-1939), fishing guide (1930-1939), fish buyer for the Boca Grande Fishery (1939-1985), and an agent for a local taxidermist. Tom's parents were Calley Boyd from Myakka, Florida, and Thomas A. Parkinson from Parkers Island, North Carolina. Tom's father came to Charlotte Harbor in the early 1890s by box car to join the commercial fishing industry. Tom married Mary Vickers from Charlotte Harbor, Florida, in 1939. Her grandfather was Kelly Falkner, who lived on the Falkner's Mound on south Cayo Costa. As a boy, Tom fished with his father, who had a fish camp on a key at the entrance to Bull Bay. Tom told me his father had worked for a Captain Smith on a sailing sloop named "Florida" in the 1890s. According to archaeologist Frank Hamilton Cushing's diary on his first trip to Key Marco in 1895, they left Punta Gorda aboard the sailing sloop "Florida" with Captain Smith and a Mr. Parkerson [sic] and visited sites on the Cape Haze Peninsula (Gilliland 1989:45). Tom's father would have been very familiar with these sites, since they were located in his fishing area. He frequently visited John Quiet, who farmed on the mound which bears his name in Turtle Bay. Eric Danielson of "Eric's Camp" (1930-1960), located on the Turtle Bay III site, was married to Tom's adopted sister, Jessie Gramm. Tom quit school when he was fifteen and moved to Boca Grande where he fished commercially and guided.

In 1939 he started working for Walter Gault's Gasparilla Fishery in Placida. Tom was assigned to manage the Boca Grande Fishery, then located at the end of the east dock off the south end of the Gasparilla Inn golf course. He was to manage the fishery for more than forty-six years. He served as the local agent for Ike Shaw Taxidermist Company of Fort Myers for more than fifty years. After retirement, Tom had been a fixture at the fish house so long that he still showed up at the dock every day. He often said, "I worked for this company without missing a day and that included weekends and holidays." Once a customer asked Tom if the fish he was selling was fresh. He slowly turned around and said, "Don't you know that anyone who would sell you a bad fish would lie to you?" He resided in Boca Grande until he died in January, 1994, at the age of 79. With him went a large piece of unwritten knowledge of Charlotte Harbor and its people.

Alfonso "Fonso" Darna

(Photo, 1993, by Bob Edic.)

Fonso Darna was born in 1910 on Cayo Costa. He is a commercial fisherman and a tarpon bait fisherman. His family was one of the last to leave Cayo Costa. He moved in 1958 to Boca Grande, where he now resides. His grandparents were Tariva and Laini "Juanita" Padilla, pioneer fisherfolk of Cayo Costa (circa 1870). His parents were Jake Darna and Sophie Padilla, also from Cayo Costa. He has always been "a commercial mullet fisherman" and is one of the last to fish commercially on Boca Grande. During tarpon season he catches "squirrel fish" for bait. I had the opportunity to mullet fish with Fonso several times in the early 1980s and cherish the experience.

Richard Coleman

(Photo, 1993, by Dick Coleman.)

Richard Coleman was born on Cayo Costa in 1913. He was a commercial fisherman (1925-1984) and fishing guide (1935-1994). Mr. Coleman was a boat captain, licensed in 1931. His great-grandparents were Tariva and Laini "Juanita" Padilla. His grandparents were Frank Toledo and Sophie Padilla. His parents were Walter Coleman and Nona Toledo. They all were from Cayo Costa. Mr. Coleman died in October, 1994 in Boca Grande.

William "Bill" Hunter

(Photo, 1990, by Bob Edic.)

Bill Hunter was born in Live Oak, Florida in 1907 and raised in Boca Grande. His father was Joseph Charles "J.C." Hunter. His grandfather was a fisherman and trader from Chokoloskee, Florida. Bill was a commercial fisherman, fishing guide, hunting guide, and netmaker. He guided for many of the area's rich and famous. He has lived on Cayo Costa and North Captiva and presently lives in Englewood, Florida.

Raymond Lowe, Sr.

(Photo, ca. 1986, courtesy of Boca Beacon.*)*

Raymond Lowe was born in 1916 at Gasparilla Village and lived on Gasparilla Island all his life. He was a commercial fisherman and boat-builder. His father, Thomas Lowe, Sr., worked at Peacons Cove circa 1889. His brother, Albert Lowe, was born at Peacons Cove. Mr. Lowe died on July 9, 1995.

Nellie (Spearing) Coleman

(Photo, 1995, by Bob Edic.)

Nellie Coleman was born in Grove City, Florida in 1918. She lived in Gasparilla Village (1925-1928) and Cayo Costa (1928-1970) and moved to Bokeelia on Pine Island in 1970. She fished and repaired nets all her life. Her late husband, Arthur "Budd" Coleman, also lived and fished on Cayo Costa.

Nellie Coleman and her dog, "Stinker," unloading fish at Punta Blanca fish house, circa late 1940s. (Photo courtesy of Nellie Coleman.)

*Esperanza Woodring talks with Bob Edic on her front
porch during her interview. (Photo, 1990, by Karen Walker.)*

Esperanza (Almas) Woodring

*Esperanza Woodring, shown net-fishing in 1949. (Photo © J.
Charles McCullough, used by permission.)*

Esperanza Woodring was born in 1901 on Cayo Costa. She was the granddaughter of
Tariva and Laini "Juanita" Padilla of Cayo Costa. Her parents were Manuel Almas and
Rosa Padilla of Cayo Costa. She married Sam Woodring, also a fisherman, of Sanibel.
They moved to Woodring Point on Sanibel Island. Esperanza fished commercially and
was a noted sport-fishing guide on Sanibel Island for many years. She died in 1992 on
Sanibel Island.

Arthur George "Bo" Smith

(Photo, ca. 1990, courtesy of Tim Smith.)

Bo Smith was born in Punta Gorda in 1929. He was a commercial fisherman (1940-1965) and a sport-fishing guide (1945-1991) renowned for tarpon fishing. His parents were Walter Smith, a merchant marine, and Thelma Barnhill, who was born in Fort Myers. He moved to Boca Grande as a boy and lived with his grandmother, Laura Barnhill, who ran the "Cozy Kitchen" restaurant. He married Billie Jean Polk from Boca Grande. He died in 1991 in Boca Grande.

Fishing in a tarpon tournament in Boca Grande Pass, ca. 1990, Arthur "Bo" Smith (center, with hands raised) prepares to release a smaller tarpon to fight another day. (Photo courtesy of Boca Beacon.*)*

Eugene "Grady" Sands

(Photo, 1990, by Jim Everidge.)

Grady Sands is a commerical fisherman and has been employed with the Gasparilla Fishery in Placida, Florida since 1938. He presently lives in Placida. Grady was born in Gasparilla Village. His father was Eugene Ivan Sands, a fisherman from Key West who came up to work at Gasparilla Village. His mother was "Aunt Mary" Sands, a midwife who delivered many babies in Charlotte Harbor's fishing communities. Grady lived on Big Mound Key with his parents from 1934 to 1937. There they fished and took care of a key lime grove for Jerome Fugate of nearby Boca Grande. Grady married Effie Mae Osteen from Lakeland, Florida.

Grady Sands

(Photo, 1991, by Bob Edic.)

Grady Sands (right) on the way to Big Mound Key for oral history interview. He is shown as a passenger on an airboat piloted by Craig Blocker, law enforcement officer for the Department of Natural Resources, Charlotte Harbor State Reserve and Aquatic Preserve.

Perry Padilla

(Photo, 1992, courtesy of Boca Beacon.*)*

Perry Padilla was born in 1912 on Cayo Costa to John Padilla, son of Tariva and Juanita Padilla. He has been a commercial fisherman all his life. He helped identify the people in the Padilla family picture taken on Cayo Costa, ca. 1901, which is used with his permission (see Chapter 5). He now resides in Boca Grande.

Eunice Albritton

*Eunice Albritton was born in Gasparilla Village.
Her father, Walter Gault, was the last proprietor of
the fishery at Gasparilla Village and founder of the
Gasparilla Fishery in Placida. Her mother was
Louise Cole, daughter of Gus Cole. Eunice and her
family have owned and managed the Gasparilla
Fishery since her father's death in 1978. She was
very helpful in providing names of senior fisherfolk
and reviewing oral histories. Many of the photo-
graphs in this book are from her extensive collection.*

(Photo, 1992, courtesy of Boca Beacon.*)*

(Photo, 1994, by Bob Edic.)

Elmer Johnson

Elmer Johnson was born on Mound Key in Estero Bay. He is the grandson of Frank Johnson and Mary White "Molly" Whitten, who settled on Mound Key in the 1870s. His grandmother Molly was a midwife and herbal healer. She was renowned throughout the area for her secret cures gathered from the wilds. His grandfather Frank was a fisherman with a colorful reputation in the area. They gained a deed for the island in 1891 signed by president Benjamin Harrison.

John Frank "Hub" Johnson, Elmer's father, was born on Mound Key in 1882. He also was a fisherman. He married Mary Hamilton from Everglades City. They lived with his grandmother, Molly, known throughout the area as "Granny." Mound Key was sold by Granny in her last years (1932) for $1,000.

Mary H. Weeks

(Photo, 1994, by Bob Edic.)

Mary "Mamie" (Hall) Weeks was born in Georgia and came to Florida in 1925 at age 14. Her parents, William T. and Mary S. Hall, were farmers.

She married Draine H. Weeks, Sr., a commercial fisherman from Bonita Springs. They lived on the mound on Coconut Point for several years. In 1945, they started Weeks Fish Camp at Estero Bay, which she and her family still run today.

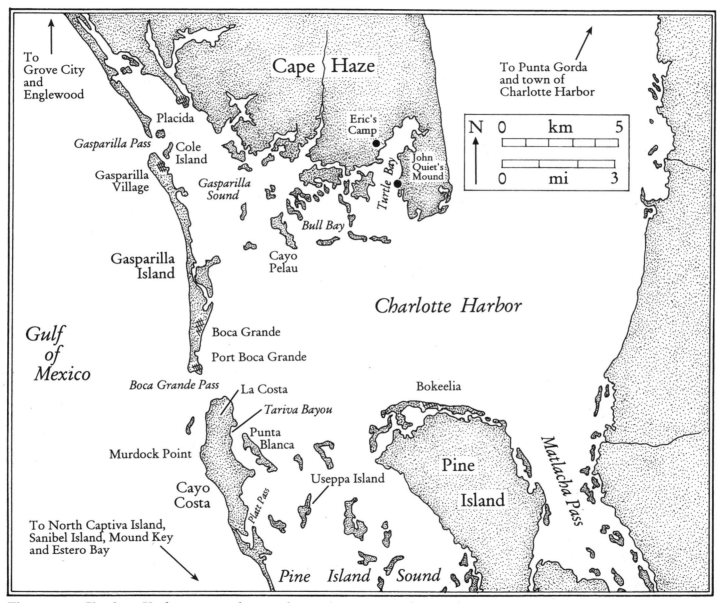

The western Charlotte Harbor area and some places often mentioned in this book. (Drawing by Merald Clark.)

The Padilla family of Cayo Costa, circa 1901.

(Photo courtesy of Perry Padilla.)

CHAPTER 5

A Pioneer Fishing Community

Oral histories of senior fisherfolk from Cayo Costa (also known as "La Costa") reveal the natural and cultural heritage of this special island. The story of the pioneer fishing families of the southwest

Florida coast and the history of Cayo Costa are deeply connected. Cayo Costa, a seven-mile-long barrier island bordering Pine Island Sound, saw the establishment of fish ranchos by the 1850s or earlier (Gibson 1982:30-32). Fishing centered on the taking and curing of mullet for the Cuban markets. Not for the weak-willed or gregarious, life for the pioneer fisherfolk closely followed the natural cycles of weather, tides, and mullet.

Perhaps the most colorful figure to arise from this milieu was Tariva Padilla, a native of the Canary Islands who founded a fishery on Cayo Costa in the 1870s and later allegedly smuggled aguardiente or "fire water" (Gibson 1982:53).

> United States Senate
> Washington, D.C.
> February 13, 1902
>
> Hon. Elihu Root,
> Secretary of War,
> Washington, D.C.
>
> My dear Sir:
>
> In order to break up smuggling in the waters about La Costa Island, Florida, an order was recently made by the Treasury Department commanding squatters on the Government reservation there to vacate. The execution of the order, I understand, was put into the hands of the commandant at Key West. Among those to whom the order would apply was Mr. Peter Nelson, postmaster at Bocagrande, a pilot, and a man who, I understand was not implicated in smuggling in any way and had not been suspected by the Government of being concerned in it. I took the matter up with the Treasury Department and there it was intimated that there would be no objection if Mr. Nelson should be allowed to remain, for awhile at least, but, I was informed that the matter was now in the hands of the War Department. I write therefore, to recommend that Mr. Nelson be allowed to remain on the reservation, inasmuch as he is a Government official and, as postmaster, is a convenience to those in the Light House and Quarantine service of the government now there.
>
> Very truly yours,
> Jas. P. Salisperero (?)

> Bocagrande, Fla.
> April 12, 1902
>
> Peter Leary Jr.,
> Major, Artillary Corps,
> Commanding Post.
> Sir,
> Yours of the 4th inst. to hand. In reply will say that Torriva Padella and family of twenty-four persons, have not left here. They have moved about three quarters of a mile south of their old place and are conducting their business the same as usual. I have good reasons to believe they are still on the reservation, but the line should be re-established by a U.S. surveyor.
>
> Respectfully,
>
> Pete Nelson
> Postmaster

Tariva and his wife Laini ("Juanita") and their family were forcibly removed from the military reservation on the northern tip of Cayo Costa ("La Costa") in 1901 for smuggling. They returned a few years later to the central area of the island where family members fished and lived until the 1970s. The modern visitor to the area, now Cayo Costa State Park, can

Portrait of the Tariva Padilla Clan, circa 1901.

Key: (1) "Phalo" Raphael Padilla (son); (2) "Augustine" Augustino Castilla (boarder); (3) "Juanita" Laini (Parez) Padilla (wife); (4) Andrew Padilla (son); (5) "Captain Pappy" Tariva Padilla (husband; head ranchero); (6) John M. Roach (owner of Useppa Island), or F.P. Roach (listed in 1900 census as a farmer on Useppa); (7) Lola (Aquilar) Padilla (granddaughter); (8) Tony Padilla (eldest son); (9) "Charcoal Maker's widow," not identified by name; (10) John Padilla (son, Perry Padilla's father); (11) Lizzie Padilla (daughter-in-law); (12) Dinna (Lizzie's sister); (13) Sam Woodring (boarder); (14) Rosa Padilla (daughter, Esperanza's mother); (15)Esperanza (Almas) Woodring (granddaughter); (16) not identified; (17) Nona (Toledo) Coleman (granddaughter, Richard Coleman's mother); (8) "Bad John" Johnnie Padilla (grandson); (19) Frank Toledo (grandson); (20) "Stella" Estella Toledo (granddaughter); (21) "Tony" Antonia Padilla (grandson); (22) Annie Butts (adopted granddaughter).

(Identifications by Perry Padilla, Alfonso Darna, and Richard Coleman.)

(Photo courtesy of Perry Padilla.)

Office of the Engineer Officer,
Key West Barracks, Fla.,
June 18th 1902
The Adjutant,
Key West Barracks, Fla.

Sir,

In compliance with the seventh paragraph of a letter of instructions, Office Post Commander, Key West Barracks, Fla., dated June 10th 1902, I have the honor to make the following report of operations conducted under instructions contained in the above mentioned letter, Office Post Commander, Key West Barracks, Fla., dated June 10th 1902, and under paragraph 1, G.O., 33, Office Post Commander, Key West Barracks, Fla., dated June 10th 1902;

At seven o'clock on the morning of June 11th, 1902, a detachment, armed and equipped, consisting of two non-commissioned officers and eight men, under my command, boarded the U.S.S. "McLane," R.C.S. and at one o'clock the same date this steamer sailed for La Costa Island, (Boca Grande), Florida, arriving at anchor in Charlotte Harbor, near the end of the above mentioned island, at 9:05 A.M., June 12th 1902- at the place marked with a star on the plat accompanying this report.

After a conference with Captain A.P.R. Hanks, R.C.S., Commanding the U.S.S. "McLane," it was decided to take a boat and proceed to the island and along its shore towards the south to a place where one Pardella, smuggler, had been located, and after reconnoitering this place to proceed further in the southerly direction until the end of the reservation was reached. At the place above mentioned, which is marked "A", on the plat accompanying this report, was a landing consisting of a lighter placed broad side on the beach with a few planks from it to shore to serve as a walk to get ashore. The building at this place had been partly burned and there was no evidence to show that they had been recently occupied. Here I was informed by one who represented himself to be Peter Nelson, Pilot, that the smugglers had left and that no one was on the island except himself and a mail carrier.

I then proceeded to a point marked "B" on the accompanying plat. One Platt had built a house here and had cleared some land. This being near the reported resort of the smugglers, that is the place to which they had moved after leaving the place marked "A", the detachment was landed and a sergeant and four privates were sent by land to the resort with instructions to arrest all persons seen and bring them to me. I then proceeded to find out if the house of Platt was occupied. To accomplish this a window was forced open. The house was found in good condition, furnished, and had the appearance of being recently occupied. At this time the sergeant, sent in the direction of the resort of the smugglers, reported with a man who gave his name as Soule and represented himself to be the mail carrier. After questioning him to some length the following was ascertained; that he had been living on the island since September, 1901, and during this time he had performed his duties as mail carrier; that Mr. Platt and wife had occupied the house above referred to, very recently but had a few days before moved to the south end of the island where they had built a house; that he was at this time occupying one of the houses formerly occupied by the smugglers. Not having any means at this time of verifying the above, I directed that Soule be held until the same could be accomplished.

I then proceeded by boat with two men, directing Sergeant Howard to take four men and proceed by land, the second resort of the smugglers marked "C" on plat accompanying this report, leaving at Platt's house a corporal and two men to further investigate the surroundings. At this place there was a small wharf, extending about thirty feet into the stream, suitable for landing small boats, and three houses built of rough pine boards stripped with shingled roofs. These houses were not furnished, except one room which was occupied by Soule, but showed signs of having been recently vacated. A clearing of about two acres surrounded the house about which was very thick underbrush composed mainly of mangroves. On the south side of the clearing was the head of a swamp as shown on the plat. Trails ran in every direction through the underbrush. Following one of these, I came to a small meadow part of which was fenced in by placing palmetto logs, cut from surrounding trees, one upon another to the height of three.

In the area fenced could be seen the remains of various plants, showing that at one time it had been cultivated. Returning to the houses, I embarked with my detachment, taking with me Soule, and boarded the "McLane" at or about 12 o'clock noon. At one o'clock I proceeded with Lieot Buhner, R.C.S., to the north end of La Costa Island where the pilots were located. Here we were met by Peter Nelson, pilot, and taking a small building near the beach used as the post office I inspected Peter Nelson's commission as postmaster and the authority for the employment of Soule to carry the mail, finding both of these genuine, I released Soule. I then questioned Peter Nelson with the following result; that the gang of Pardella, smuggler, consisted of twenty five, that the men of this gang had left La Costa Island the Sunday preceeding (June 8th); that the women of this party had left the island about two weeks before; that the men had left two boats, one the "Pigeon", the other, a small schooner, not named, for Belle Air, Fla., where the whole gang now is; that the second resort of the smugglers had been built and occupied by one Martin, who had cleared the land and built the houses thinking at the time he was far enough south to be off the military reservation; that the pilots and their families generally living on the north end of the island were as follows,

I.W. Johnson, wife and three children,
W.H. Johnson, wife and three children,
Peter Nelson;

that all except himself (Peter Nelson) were in Punta Gorda; that he knew of only one "coal burner" that have ever made charcoal on the island. This man, a Cuban, whom he would recognize but did not know the name of, he thought lived in Punta Gorda.

I then proceeded to Gasparilla Island and found that the following named persons resided upon the military reservation on that island;

Light House Establishment.
William Lester, Light House Keeper
Chas. Johnson, Asst. Keeper, wife and four children—oldest seven years,
Quarantine Station.
Dr. B.B. Blount, wife and four children, Chas. N. Conolly and Archer T. Turner, Attendants.

I then returned to the "McLane".

Ist Endorsement
Headqrs. Department of the East,
Governor's Island, N.Y.,
July 1, 1902

Respectfully forwarded to the Adjutant General of the Army in connection with the instructions contained in War Department letter of May 1, 1902.

It would seem from this report that the Pardilla family and group of smugglers have removed from La Costa Island to Belle Air, Fla; that they embrace about 25 persons; and that they have left behind them one building of no value and two others, together estimated to be worth one hundred dollars.

The Commanding Officer, Key West Barracks, proposed to destroy these houses which, if left standing, will invite to a return of the gang, I recommend that a revenue cutter be sent to destroy them.

It is a condition of the residence of the pilots named herein, that they shall give notice of the return of any unathorized people to the reservation (see letter from the Commanding Officer, Key West Barracks, of April 4, 1902, copy enclosed).

No further action than that above is recommended at present.

(signature)

Major General,

Commanding

War Department
Washington,
July 18, 1902

Sir:

The Department is in receipt of a letter from the Commanding Officer at Key West Barracks dated June 23, 1902, inclosing a report from Lieut. Wm. H. Peck, Artillary Corps, of his trip to La Costa and Gasperilla Islands, Charlotte Harbor, Florida, for the purpose of expelling the Pardella gang of smugglers and making a rough survey of the La Costa Island Military Reservation, the southern boundary of which has been so marked that none can fail to see the line.

In forwarding this report, the Post Commander desires to express his appreciation of the prompt and excellent service rendered by Capt. A.P.R. Hanks and his executive officer, of the U.S. Revenue Cutter "McLane."

It appears from this report that the Pardella family have left behind them three buildings, which if left standing, will no doubt invite the return of the family to the island, and the Department Commander recommends that a revenue cutter be sent to destroy them.

Concurring with this recommendation, I beg to request such action on the part of your Department as will accomplish the desired purpose.

Very Respectfully,

The Honorable, (signature)
Secretary of War,

See photo of Peter Nelson in this chapter.

walk the well-kept nature trails past the sites of the former fishing settlements to find that nature has reclaimed most traces of the pioneer occupation (Edic 1992:221-225).

Padilla family members recount memories of early life in the fishing communities on Cayo Costa. Refer to the Padilla family tree (page 78) to understand relationships among people mentioned by these informants. John Padilla, his wife, and daughter are in the boat in the cover photograph.

Selected descendants of Tariva Padilla, called "Captain Pappy,"
Head Fish Ranchero, 1870s - 1910, and Laini ("Juanita") Parez.

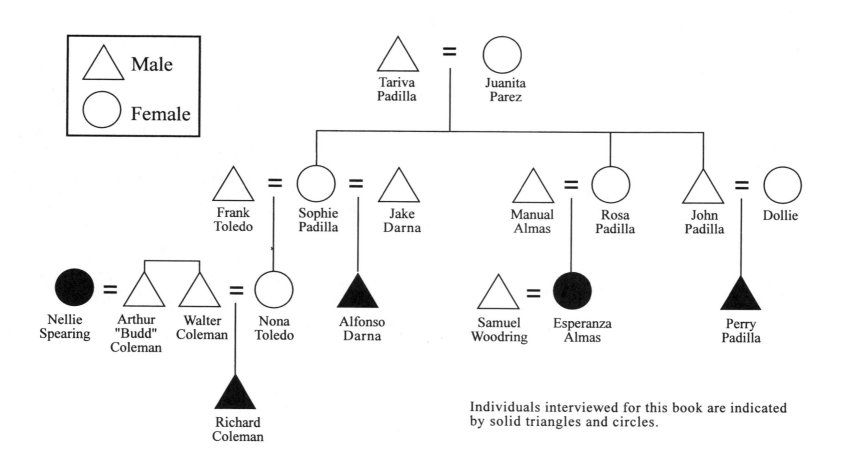

Individuals interviewed for this book are indicated
by solid triangles and circles.

Richard Coleman

Old Man [Tariva] Padilla came to this country, but how in the hell he ever came here I will never know. He was from the Canary Islands. The old lady ["Juanita," his wife] was from Mexico. Old Man Tariva Padilla ran that big mullet business [here]. He lived at the north end of Cayo Costa [locally called "La Costa"] on that bayou. Tariva Bayou is what they call it. Tariva [my great-grandfather] had a crew there that would catch the fish. I think he had twenty or twenty-five men. He did not do the fishing himself. He was a boss. He would see that they were split and salted, and all of that.

They told me the way they did it. They would get these mangrove poles and put about six of them together about twenty-five feet high. Then they put a tarp over the top of them. They would put a fellow in it. If he saw a bunch of mullet down there, he would start waving a sheet or something. Then another one up here would see it. He would see it, and the other one would wave it. They would be down there somewhere with a seine, and they would haul all of the fish ashore. I do not know for sure, but I think that five-thousand pounds of mullet would have been a hell of a lot of mullet back in those days [in one haul]. They would split them and take them back to their ranches. The crew were mostly Spanish or Cuban. They would put them [the mullet] in these schooners and take them to Cuba. They would trade a lot of them for whiskey and provisions. He would trade the fish in Cuba for liquor and would get a little money. He would bring that back over here. In 1902 that is the reason the government moved them all off, because there was smuggling.

I am talking about times back when they did not have any motorboats. There were no motorboats [here] whatsoever until 1910. Then we began to get some motorboats.

◆ ◆ ◆

Kelly Falkner ("Old Man Falkner") with children Fred and Nellie. Nellie was the mother of Mary Parkinson, wife of Tom Parkinson, who ran the Boca Grande Fishery (see page 54).

[Old Man Falkner lived on the south end of Cayo Costa]. All he had there was bee hives, and that is what he lived on. He did not even fish. He lived off of those bees. I guess he took most of it back to the mainland. I was a pretty young kid then. I do not know how long, but he was there a long time.

Well, I will tell you those hogs [on Cayo Costa] are damn good, I thought. The fat on the one that we killed was two inches thick. They were there years and years ago. There used to be some down at Captiva, but they killed them all off. I do not know why they [the State] wanted to kill them. There were deer [there] also, but they killed them all off. Most of them were big deer. The last of them, I think, swam to Pine Island, most of the big ones. You'd see one swim across there now and then.

Walter Coleman [was my father]. [His brothers were] Arthur, Shelly, Orlando, and Eugene. Dollie was my daddy's sister. She married Old Man John Padilla, who is buried on Cayo Costa. Eugene was shot [accidentally, by Esperanza Woodring] with a 22-caliber rifle when he was young, about five years old. He lived to be about twenty-one years old. It began to give him trouble, and he went up to Arcadia. They operated on him there. That night it seemed like a blood vessel got busted, and he just bled to death. He died right there in Arcadia hospital. He is buried way up there on the hill by Captain Peter Nelson, my dad, his mother, and all of them...[I had] just one [brother], Woodrow. He got killed in an auto accident. My mother's name was Nona [Toledo] [Sophie Padilla's daughter]. [She was] ninety-two, I guess [when she died].

◆ ◆ ◆

Well, you know, in 1910 they buried a lot of people there [in the old grave yard]. The quarantine station was on the north point of Cayo Costa and [had] a dock going out there. That was before it was at Boca Grande. You would receive the load of phosphate over there. On the bay side. It had a breakwater there—two rows of pilings with rock in between them. You could go around there and get in that thing, and it was always calm, no matter how rough it was on the outside. Of course, it was government. You were not supposed to get in there, but we did. That was right there at north point...there was rock on the bottom, coquina rock. They are all about gone now; there are only a few left there. Then going south, on Cayo Costa Island, there are some mangroves. It used to make a big cove in there [Old Place Hole]. At one time—way back in 1910—across from Useppa Island before you got to Pelican Bay where we go in at [now]—there was a separate pass there that you could go right in Pelican Bay. "Old Place Hole" is what they called it. Old Place Hole has about twenty feet of water in it in places. You could go right in through there. We always went in that way. Then finally it filled in there, and it broke through at Pelican Pass and went around the other way, right where Deadman's Key broke in. If I had a map, I could probably show you. Nell [Padilla] Adams's father, John Padilla, was the last one to be buried there. Old man Tariva's son [John] was buried there in the 1930s. Nell Adams was old man John Padilla's daughter. She was born and raised on Cayo Costa. Old man John, old man Tony, Bevo Padilla, and Phalo Padilla [were Tariva's sons]. Rosa [and Sophie were] his daughters.

◆ ◆ ◆

It was 1937, I guess it was, when he [John Padilla] was buried over there at Cayo Costa. He died over there at Cayo Costa. He was fishing.

About two o'clock in the afternoon me and a fellow by the name of Neil Lanair were there. I said, "Neil, they are having old man John Padilla's funeral over there at Tariva Bayou [today]. You and I should go over there to it." He said okay so we got into the boat. We went over there and ran the bow of the boat on the beach. We did not put any anchor or anything out; we just ran it up there. They were up there preaching the funeral then, and we run up to where they had him buried. You could see the bow of my boat. I eyed it every now and then. Louis Darna and Gilbert Joiner dug the grave down there. Jack Griffinhoff worked for Van Patten. He is the one that handled the funeral and all. And Mrs. Cecilia Gaines, Edgar Gaines' mother, preached the funeral. There were a lot of oak trees and cabbages [cabbage palms] all around there. There were a lot of little ridges in there, and you could tell they were graves.

You see, old man Bevo Padilla—that was old man John Padilla and Phalo Padilla's brother—he had a sister or brother... I do not know which one it was that died that was sixteen years old. They put him in a copper tank and buried it there. I was taking Clem Johnson down to those islands near Captiva Rocks. We were coming back in one day, and he was telling me about that. He said, "Now, there is a casket in there. I thought it was something else. I dug down to it and chopped into it and saw it was a casket. I covered it back up." I said, "Are you sure that you covered it back up?" He said, "Yes." I said, "What was it made of?" "Copper," he said. I said, "You did not move it?" And he said, "No," that he did not move it. What year that he got into it, I do not know. Of course, he did not know. He thought it was something else. I told Arthur ["Budd" Coleman] one time that before he died we should go over there sometime and find it. The Bible says let the dead rest, but I said that if they ever get interested in finding it, I believe I can find it. "We will take one of these Geiger counters and find it," I said. It is right in the thickest of all those oak trees. They were little oak trees when they put in old man John. There are cabbages [palms] all around it.

◆ ◆ ◆

My dad [Walter Coleman] was over at Useppa guiding a party. We stayed out at the guide house one night. So I said, "Who is in all of those graves over there at Tariva Bayou [Old Place Hole]? It looked like about thirty of them [buried] over there." He said, "Most of them was those Cubans who were on those boats that sank in the 1910 hurricane." They sank out there on the Patricio Shoals. He said they landed up over in that cove. It was all young boys, and we did not know who in the hell they were. "Well," he said, "It would take three or four days to get to Fort Myers to the law, so we rolled them up in sails and buried them in there." I said, "Damn, there is a lot of them." Most of them that were put [buried] there were Cubans. There used to be two of them [graves] around on the west side of the island, further down there near a buttonwood tree, pretty close to the gulf. I used to know where they are, but I do not any more. The buttonwood tree is gone. I would not have the least idea where they are at....but they are out there on the west side [of Cayo Costa].

Now, Esperanza [Woodring], down here at Sanibel, is old lady Rosa [Padilla]'s daughter. She had come down there several times looking for the graves, but she could not find them. Jesse Padilla, before he died, was looking for them, and he could not find them. Louis Darna said he can go right straight to it. But I do not think Louis had the first idea where in the hell they were at [now]. I can come pretty close to it. I do not know how close, but I can come pretty damn close to it. But, you see, since old man [Gilbert] Joiner was put there, there was a big cove in there. Now it is straight; it is filled in. I heard one time that they washed out. Bell Hamilton told me that once, but I do not think so. I went over there a lot in the wintertime, and I think that if they are still there, the sand got in there and maybe blew over and covered everything up pretty well.... to where now you cannot find it. Alfonso [Darna] should come pretty close to where they are at.... he used to live there. He spent one night on the graves. I think he was coon hunting out there and got lost in those woods. He sat out there on those graves [for the night], he told me.

About three years ago, my Uncle Arthur ["Budd" Coleman] and I went to Cayo Costa. We went through those woods and went out there by that old settlement where we all used to live [on central Cayo Costa]. We had a house there, and it was all growed up. Of course, we found some old bottles and stuff and the blocks the houses were sitting on. You could not tell much about it. But we found a hibiscus tree. It was growing in his grandmother's yard, right in the corner. He said, "I'll be damned!" That thing was in full bloom and still looked good and still had flowers on it after all of them years. There were a good many houses here [then]. Of course, the old school house was down over to the left. It burned up. I remember when it burned up. That was when it used

Cayo Costa School House circa 1920s. Left to right, back row: Alfonso Darna, Henry Darna, Anna Woodhull, Lola Martin, Corrine Martin, Perry Padilla; front row: Teacher: Mrs. Woodhull, Ugenia Martin, John Martin, Louis Darna, Nell Padilla, Laura Woodring, Joe Darna. (Photo courtesy of Nellie Coleman. Identifications by Alfonso Darna.)

to be at Cayo Costa. Then they moved the school to Punta Blanca. They used one of those houses over there for the school and just left the one at Cayo Costa. But they had been going to school at Punta Blanca before it burned up.

Alfonso Darna

[Frank] Toledo was [my mother's] first husband. Then she married a [Jake] Darna, then Rodriguez.

[There were] plenty of pigs! You know those pigs were put there by the people that lived there. Everybody put a pig or two on there, and it was no time—they are worse than rabbits—there were hundreds of them. You see, there are a lot of oaks on that island. In the wintertime or fall, there would be a lot of acorns for them. Then [there were] these cabbage palms. You would see them rooting for these dead berries of the palms that fall down. They were grinding up the seeds—that was what you'd see them rooting for—these

dead berries of the palms that fall down; that was what the hogs were eating. You know the little cabbage berry seeds? They taste like chewing tobacco. I do not mean the outside, I mean the seed on the inside of it. Yes, they are foul. When we were kids and [were] over there, we would put a wad of them in our mouth and play like we were chewing tobacco and spit it out. It looked like a chew-tobacco spit, you know. They would be dried out, and the pigs would be eating them and grinding them up. You could see, when you butchered one, it would be ground up just like corn. You would not believe that they could pick up so many of those things. Of course, the ground would be black with them under the trees. It seems like those palm trees bear more than the palms on this island [Gasparilla]. Every one of those trees would be big bags full of them cabbage palmetto berries—all of them trees. That is what the coons and the animals over there ate.

Esperanza Woodring

I was born on Cayo Costa [Tariva's Bayou] in 1901. That is where my grandparents started out. My grandfather [Tariva Padilla] came from Canary Island. My grandmother [Laini or "Juanita" Padilla], I guess, was from Mexico. My dad, Manuel [Almas] was from Spain, I think. See, in those days the only way they [could] get from one country to another [was to] stow away. After they would leave their country, why they could not throw them overboard, so they had to take them wherever they were going. I had seven sisters and five brothers that were alive. One died. My mother [Rosa Padilla] had thirteen children all together. So now there are only four girls left and one boy. The rest of them have all passed away. Originally, my grandparents were from Cayo Costa. When I was a kid, I did not pay enough attention to that kind of stuff [until] it was too late; I was sorry I did not.

That is the school I went to [on central Cayo Costa]. Well, the first teacher that I had was named Captain Peter Nelson.

Now, I know that you have heard of him. He was a great old guy, I will tell you. [Then] they had a school house on Punta Blanca.

They did not have nothing in the markets [there]. They used to have to make everything. Well, we did too when we lived on Cayo Costa. [Do] you know what we used for clothespins? Palmetto stalks [the stem of a frond]. We would cut them about that long [10 inches] and split it. Sometimes they would hold; sometimes they would tear up.

I will tell you about my grandfather. He used to have a fishing camp down here near the lighthouse [on Sanibel]. There used to be a deep well, and all the fishermen and boatmen that came along there would go to that well to get water. They had these wooden barrels down the sides, and they would rot and cave in. So somebody would come along and put a new one in there. Years and years, until they developed that down there, that well was down there, and they called it "Tariva's Well." I could have killed them when they went and filled it in with sand and dirt. Of course, you know that was an old well, and there is lots of background to it, because that is what the fishermen de-

pended on [for] their water. He [Tariva] did not live on Sanibel. He just had his fishing camp there. He lived on Cayo Costa mostly and lower Captiva. See, these fish used to come in schools, and they would take these huge big nets and rope them in [with] seines. A great big heavy, long, and real deep seine. [They were] cotton....there was no such thing as flax in those days.

We moved from the McAdow place in 1910 to [central] Cayo Costa [by Murdock Point]. That is when they started building there. The families bought lots, and they built houses. I heard [later] that the government ran some of the families that lived there off [for smuggling], but I never heard it when I was a kid.

When my grandfather lived on Cayo Costa, I do not think that there was any other family there but just his immediate family and maybe two or three of the men who worked for him. The people who lived there were all related one way or another. I guess he was a hard-boiled old customer. [laughter] He did not like a lot of strangers around.

They used to mostly ship their fish from Key West out to Cuba. There was, I imag-

Captain Peter Nelson, Postmaster/School Teacher circa 1900. (Photo courtesy of Richard Coleman.)

ine, a special boat to come and pick them up every so often. These smacks used to have these great big huge wells in the middle of the boat, and they used to catch mostly grouper. They used to go way back out in the Gulf and fish for red grouper and black grouper. Of course, if some of the fish died, then they would salt them and hang them up and cure them. Whoever was in the family, that is the ones that worked. Once in a while, probably, there was a straggler [who was] looking for work. But they were all local people. I do not think he got any outsiders. You see, they all mostly lived like a family all together in these huge palmetto houses. They could not possibly get outsiders or strangers who they did not know. They would have to know them on account of having his daughters and his wife there. I guess they all ate together and slept in these shacks. I think he was the only one that I know of. Well, there might have been another one or two, but they did not have set fishing camps like he did.

They [the Cubans] used to have some kind [of food]. I do not know what it was. I guess it was made out of wheat because it was brown. It was like a flour, and they used to bring a lot of that in. They used

that sort of like a dessert. They put sugar and milk in it, and they used to get that from these Cuban smacks. And they would bring olive oil and knick-knacks [and] stuff like that. They traded some fish or whatever the islands used to have. I do not remember seeing any money until I was grown. Money? Nobody knew what that was. They just traded back and forth whatever they had.

The hogs on Cayo Costa were from my grandfather. He was the first one that brought them there. They just let them run wild. They had chickens and ducks and stuff like that. There might have been a few deer on the island, but if there were, they would not have killed them.

Mullet were caught in the winter when they were spawning. It would last about three months out of the year. November, December, and January. I do not think they bothered fishing [after that]. [They] probably fished enough to eat, but I do not think they did much [commercial] fishing. They probably made what they could in those three months, and then they survived with whatever they could rake and scrape out of the water: clams, oysters, and they ate a lot of fish. They also hunted birds, and maybe they killed a deer once in

awhile or something like that. But they survived entirely off of the land.

They would put them [split and cleaned mullet] down in brine. See, they had these great big wooden barrels, and they would brine them down because they keep better

Roe curing (Source: Gibson 1982:48).

Method of Curing Mullet Roes

The mullet-roes are thus cured: Having been collected from the fish in a vat with a weak solution of brine over them, and allowed thus to remain over night, the roes are taken out the next morning and carefully spread on boards in the sun. After one day's exposure, other boards are laid on the roe. They are now between boards and in a shape which will admit of rapid handling in case of rain. If the sun is shining brightly and there is a good breeze, a week will suffice for the roes to become dry and thoroughly pressed. Afterwards they are handled in baskets, tubs, &c, and are sent to market en masse. There is a greater demand for mullet-roe in Cuba than in Florida. If a spawning fish is bruised or otherwise injured in the seine the roe is worthless, turning a dark-red color. Again, if too much salt is put upon a spawning fish at first, the sac cracks and the eggs are burned out on being exposed to sun and pressure. Rain is injurious to mullet-roes hence the threat of a shower causes much uneasiness in a drying camp. (George Goode, 1844-1887)

that way. They would take the mullet and salt it real good, and then they would put them together like this [stacked and piled] because they would go in the barrels easier. Then they would ship them out. They would go down as far as Key West, and then these boats would pick it up and take them to Cuba or wherever they could get a market for them, I suppose. In those days it was all sailboats, you know. There was no such a thing as ice.

My father had a gill net. He used to mullet fish in season. Then when the season was over, he used to catch trout or redfish or whatever would sell at the market.

[We ate mostly] mullet. You can take a fisherman, and he has got all kinds of fish in his boat. If he is going to eat well once in awhile he might change, but, most of the time, what do you think he would take home to eat? Mullet. I like most any kind but a snook. I do not like snook.

Aguadin [aguardiente] was white, pure, all white. It would knock your head off if you smelled of it. I do not know how they could drink it. But I have handled a many of those [bottles], I can tell you that much.

Tariva and Juanita Padilla circa 1880. (Photo courtesy of Richard Coleman.)

I used to take fishing parties out mostly. I was a fishing guide. Not now. I have not been in a boat in three months. You do not know how I miss it. That is my boat out there [on the dock]. [Now] it is [my son] Ralph's boat, but I call it mine. See, all of that stuff is in his name, so he has to repair it and keep it up. [laughter] Well, I used to try to [commercial] fish, too, in between times. I used to net fish. I had my own net and boat [a pole skiff]. At first [I had cotton nets], then we started using flax. Then [we] eventually [switched to] nylon, and I do not like nylon very much. We generally always had three nets [for mullet]. We ordered most of ours [nets] from New York from a company. The name of them was W. A. Auger in New York. I still have some of their advertisements.

The name of the fish company from Punta Gorda was Chadwick Brothers. Then later the Punta Gorda Fish Company took it over. We had a run-boat that used to come up there in Tarpon Bay and pick up our fish. If we wanted groceries or shoes or anything, we would just write up an order and send it back on the fish boat. The next boat would bring it down. They would deduct it out of your pay. We got a little bit of money. Have you ever heard of Harry Goulding who was in Punta Gorda? He was the big shot at the Punta Gorda Fish Company. [He ran the office—kept the books, processed the fishermen's orders for groceries, etc. He used to brag that he knew the bra size of every fisherman's wife because he handled their orders to Sears Roebuck or to Montgomery Ward for clothing. (Personal Correspondence, U.S. Cleveland, May 9, 1995).] We always sent our orders and addressed our grocery stuff to him, and he would take care of it. I mean, he was really good. If it was in Punta Gorda, you got it on the next boat. I knew him personally. He was a good guy. They used to buy nets and boats and everything else for the guys. I imagine when they went out of business they lost a lot of money from debts that these fishermen had never paid out. In fact, I guess some of them did not want to pay. [laughter] And they used to own a lot of the boats that they used to fish on. [Normally the fish company owned all the skiffs the fish crews used to hold their nets and then the fish. The crew captain owned the launch that pulled them and paid all expenses. The practice was for the captain to receive one-third share for furnishing the launch, gasoline, etc. plus one-third as captain. The remaining third was divided among the fish crew equally. (Personal Correspondence, U.S. Cleveland, May 9, 1995).]

[My husband] Sam [Woodring]'s [brothers and sisters were] Anna, Carl, Alva, Flora, and Harrison. [There were] five: two girls and three boys, I guess. Grandpa Woodring came from Pennsylvania. He got married there, I guess. He used to be a blacksmith. He went from town to town fixing the wagon wheels and stuff like that. He was in the Civil War.

[I have] two ornery sons, Ralph Woodring and Preston Woodring. Preston is the oldest. Preston was in the service for twenty-five years, and then he retired and came to Sanibel and used to work at the water department. [Preston died in 1994. -R.F.E.] Ralph is a shrimper and a sportsman. He keeps that Bait Box [tackle store] down there. That is his business. My grandfather was Tariva Padilla. That was my mother's father. Tariva's sons were John, Tony, Bevo, Phalo, Rosa....and Sophie. Sophie was Richard [Coleman]'s grandmother. See, his mother [Nona] was Sophie's daughter. The Colemans are related [to me] through marriage. They married some of my mother's family.

There are five generations in our family now. [I have] nine grandchildren. [And] great-grandchildren I would have to count. [laughter] Let me see...that would be a total of nine living.

Arthur [Budd] Coleman's mother had a little boarding house. She had about five or six fishermen living with her, and they paid her, I think, $20 a month for room and board. I used to go and help her wash and scrub all day long for twenty-five cents a day. Gosh. I do not know how I lived.

See, when you are a kid, you do not listen to all of this. It just goes whisp. Then, when it is too late, you wished you had listened to a whole lot of that stuff.

Nellie Coleman

The government took them [the Padillas] off there [Cayo Costa] for smuggling and stuff like that [in 1902]. I was just a kid at that time [when I first heard about it]. I wasn't born 'til 1918. In the 18th century, they [the Spanish] was hauling the black people over from Africa; they had smuggling there even then. They had the people that had money and the people that didn't, and the ones that didn't had to get out and scratch to get the money. So they got rum from Bimini. Toward the last [of prohibition], they started enforcing it in the 1930s. We didn't get rich; we just got by.

The Padillas taught my husband a lot of things [about fishing], but they never told him nothing about the Indians. I suppose they had all gone to the Everglades by the time the Padillas got in here [in the 1870s].

[I lived on Cayo Costa]. I was brought over there in 1928. My father [George Spearing] was raised there. He was born in north Florida same as [my husband] "Budd" [Arthur Coleman]. The Colemans and the Spearings came from the same place. Walter [Coleman], his mother and his youngest brother [Eugene], and old Captain [Peter] Nelson is buried there [in the historic cemetery].

I was born in Grove City [Florida]. Then when I was three months old, we moved to Cedar Key, and I was raised in Cedar Key 'til I was seven years old. Then we came back down here [Gasparilla Village]. It wasn't easy, even in 1928 'til the 30s [on Cayo Costa]. We was raised on swamp cabbage, gopher turtles, and cornbread. We ate most anything we could, but I liked pompano. After my dad started pompano fishing, that was one of my favorite fish, but we ate anything we could get. We even caught those little pinfish with a pin hook. They had hard times then, too. They could eat the fish and stuff like that, but they didn't have hard cash.

We went to school on Punta Blanca. The school house was there. I've got some pictures of it. I remember seeing it as a kid, down where the building was in Pelican Bay. I've got some pictures of some of us in front of the old school house before Collier had it pumped in. See, you could walk underneath the school house before they pumped it in. Then you couldn't even get under it. It wasn't so far off the ground then when they pumped Punta Blanca in. When they dug that channel around there, they pumped it in on the island and built the island up 'cause the tide went across it.

I've been mending nets all my life. I've hung them, had my own nets and boats and everything else 'til we moved over here [to Bokeelia].

There was a lot of families living there [on Cayo Costa] at times. About twenty years ago [1970], we moved over here [Bokeelia].

Well, they began to make laws that hurt the commercial fisherman. You couldn't catch this, and you couldn't catch that. You look in your Bible, it says that fishermen are the most independent there was. They didn't like anybody saying what to do. The disciples told them what to do, when they came across them. They had to, that was their job. The fishermen was the last ones to follow them; they wanted to be independent [even then]. That's how it was on Cayo Costa.

Hurricanes have influenced the marine and estuarine environments and the lives of Charlotte Harbor's fisherfolk. This photograph shows stilt houses at Gasparilla Village blown over by the 1921 hurricane. (Photo courtesy of Janice Busby.)

CHAPTER 6

Natural Forces

Seasons

The annual cycles of the year in the Charlotte Harbor area are marked by four changes in prevailing weather patterns. These all directly affect the estuarine environment and the availability of certain marine species. Both the aboriginal and historic fisherfolk, whose livelihoods were based on these resources, could predict many of these events and use them to their advantage. Environmental research indicates that these weather patterns generally have been present for the past six thousand years in southwest Florida (Upchurch et al. 1992:69-70).

Fish migrations are weather-related. Certain species of fishes, such as mangrove snapper, sawfish, kingfish, and tarpon, which require warmer waters, frequent Charlotte Harbor only when water conditions are warm and leave the area as water cools. The reverse is true of species that require cooler waters: bluefish, sailors' choice, and flounder (Storey 1937:11-22). These species can be used as seasonal indicators by archaeologists.

Prevailing wind patterns are also seasonal and were important to the aboriginal traveler. Daily and seasonal fluctuations of winds determine when, and in what direction, transportation by water can be safely and efficiently achieved. Thus winds influence daily life and seasonal trade patterns.

July–September

Starting with the hot rainy season, July through September, high temperatures average in the nineties and prevailing winds blow from the south, heavy with warm, moist air and occasional tropical storms and hurricanes. The prevailing southerly winds flood Charlotte Harbor with prolonged high tides, especially when amplified by lunar effects of the full and new moon. These high tides of summer allow boat access to places in the shallow estuaries that are not accessible during the winter months. Travel by boat to points north is facilitated, but summer storms can make travel dangerous if boats are caught in open waters.

October–November

Prevailing winds turn toward the east, marking the end of the rainy season. This warm, dry season lasts until cold fronts make their way farther down the Florida peninsula, bringing with them occasional rains, cooler temperatures, and the first northwesters of the season.

December–March

Stronger cold fronts with lower temperatures and high winds occur more frequently from the end of November to March. Water travel in a southerly direction is made much easier under these prevailing conditions. Northerly winds also prevent tidal build-up through the Straits of Florida into the Gulf of Mexico. Gulf waters are held back, and much of Charlotte Harbor's remaining water is blown out to the Gulf. Extreme low tides prevail in the estuaries, depending on lunar events. Tides sometimes remain low for days at a time. Watercraft caught in the shallows of the estuary can remain aground until conditions change.

Temperatures can fall to the low thirties at night but usually recover quickly as the sun rises. Prevailing low temperatures can cause the shallow water in the harbor to drop below fifty degrees. This can cause fish kills among some species and paralyze others, making them easy to gather in large quantities (Storey 1937:22).

April–June

March brings west winds in mornings that swing south and then east toward evening. This makes travel from the outer islands to the mainland easiest in the earlier part of the day, with return trips to the west a late afternoon event. Cold fronts rarely reach this far south in this season. Warm moderate temperatures prevail as winds turn southerly. By the end of June, summer thunderstorms and hot humid subtropical weather return.

During my interviews with the senior fisherfolk, I asked about seasonal weather changes and availability of certain fish and shellfish through the year.

Tom Parkinson

I do not think it would be too hard [to predict tidal episodes]. You just figure your spring tides [based on the phases of the moon], and you figure your weather along with your spring tides, and you can tell. With a heavy northwester—you get low, low tides.

We put the nets out at high tide, and the fish would be trapped in the potholes when it all went dry.

Bill Hunter

I eat oysters in January, February, and March. Oysters are through spawning [then], and they are fat. By the middle of March they [oysters] are full of roe themselves, so I don't bother with them. I eat clams all the time except them months [January, February, and March]; clams are spawning then. Scallops were the best in August, September, and October. I fished redfish May, June, and July. I only fished the times when they were there. If they were not there, I did not fish. Redfish spawn in July, August, and September. I have caught a lot of trout in the summer; there are more that spawn in the summer than the winter; they seem to spawn all year around. [I would catch the most grouper in] July, August, and September; after September, the northwesters would begin to come down. I never found a roe in any of them.

Alfonso Darna

In roe season [in the fall] I would fish [mullet] going out the passes [when they run, on the northwesters]. Then in the summer, it [the fishing] would be all in the bay.

You get kingfish in the early part of October and November, you catch them [with hand lines] out here off the sea buoy [Boca Grande Pass]. It seems like in the fall they are going south; and in the spring [when they return], they are going north. The silver mullet is in fat season now [February]; they will have roe in March and April. That is their season to spawn.

Richard Coleman

We never did get many shellfish in the fall. In the winter time we'd get some oysters, maybe clams.

Kingfish would never come in here until the fifteenth of March [on their way north]. Then they would get here about the tenth of October [on their way south]. Weather has a lot to do with it.

Raymond Lowe, Sr.

Winter freezes kills a lot of snook off. Roe season for snook is in June and July.

Pompano were caught in the spring when the mullet spawn out. Sometimes they don't show up [weather-related]. In the spring they could be counted on.

Esperanza Woodring

We survived the rest of the year on [what we made from] the winter catch of mullet. After roe season, they were the easiest fish to catch. We would catch some just to eat.

Bo Smith

Some years would be a good year, and the next year would be a bad year for mullet. You only get them right ahead of the fronts. Seems like every year [in the summer] grouper fishing, why you'd catch a thousand/fifteen hundred pounds a day.

You started [mullet fishing] around Halloween or Thanksgiving, you could catch a few around. Then they'd get in bigger bunches like in November, December, and January.

Clams are good all year round. In summertime clams are better. Now oysters—

you don't get them 'til you get two or three cold spells on them. A lot of people go to get them [too early], but they're just wasting them, you know. If you wait 'til the water gets pretty cold, then they get fat.

I guided for McMillan for twenty-five years and always had them February and March 'til the 15th of April. Then you'd always take two weeks off in April to get your boat ready for tarpon season [in] May, June, and July. Then you'd go grouper fishing.

Winter Freezes

Sudden, unseasonably cold weather can cause water temperature to plummet rapidly in the shallow depths of the estuaries in Charlotte Harbor. Certain species of fish that do not tolerate cold water are weakened or killed.

Longer durations of low temperatures can cause large fish kills. The massive waters of the Gulf of Mexico, which are not as readily affected by sudden drops in temperature, serve as a refuge for fish that otherwise would have been trapped in the shallows. It would be more disastrous if water temperatures in the Gulf dropped significantly, even for a short period.

Sam Woodring, Esperanza Woodring's husband, was an informant for Storey and Gudger's article, "Mortality of Fishes Due to Cold at Sanibel Island, Florida: 1886-1936" (1936:641). Sam recounts elder fisherfolk as calling the winter of 1886 the worst that had ever been known. Another local fisherman, George Underhill, stated that on De-

Dennis and Darlene Edic with a snook he caught by hand during a freeze in 1981. (Photo by Bob Edic.)

Freezes

January is the coldest month of the year, during which mean temperatures range from 60°-63° F over the study region. During this month, and less often in December, freezes may occur in southwest Florida. Since 1900 there have been at least 12 "freezes" reported in some part of the region. The Southwest Florida Water Management District stated that "frost in southwest Florida is most likely on cold, calm nights (maximum radiational cooling) with more frequent occurrences in low-lying areas" and "damage to crops and citrus is most severe when lingering temperatures, below freezing, occur throughout the night and those low temperatures are combined with a strong northwest wind so that penetration of cold is at a maximum."

In addition to agricultural losses, freezes cause mortality among mangroves; sublethal frost damage also causes the loss of fruit and propagules from mangroves. Freezes kill or burn seagrasses and cause widespread mortality among fishes and some invertebrates.

(Excerpted from Estevez, et al. 1984:R-31).

cember 29-30, 1894, temperatures dropped to a low of twenty-eight degrees and the cold lasted for a night and a day. He claimed this was even more destructive than the freeze of 1886. In addition to vast quantities of shallow-water fish that were killed, many species of Gulf fish were also killed. Some of the prevalent species reported killed included tarpon, gafftopsail catfish, lane snapper, pinfish, silver mullet, permit, sharks, and jewfish. Usually these freezes are accompanied by cold fronts with northerly winds, as evidenced by Underhill's statement: "...the tide went out and stayed out for three days." Even coastal trees, such as buttonwood and red and white mangroves, were killed back to their main limbs.

Winter freezes could provide a short-term surplus of easily captured fish that could be preserved to get through the catastrophe. From personal experience in Charlotte Harbor in the winter of 1981, water temperatures dropped to fifty degrees for a few days, resulting in a massive fish kill in the bays. Large jack crevalles and snook with a translucent white spot in the center of their heads from the cold floundered on the surface. These fish were easily caught with a dip net. As the water temperatures rose over the next couple of days, some recovered, but many died.

The absence of certain animal and plant species recovered from local archaeological excavations can indicate cooler climatic episodes in the past. Certain fishes—such as snook, lane snapper, mangrove snapper, permit, and needlefish—are on their northern limits in Florida (Storey 1937:12-15). Longer and more frequent periods of cooler temperatures could have forced some species to warmer waters south of the area temporarily during these episodes. Absence of certain species of plants, such as gumbo-limbo trees, can indicate longer cooler periods.

Raymond Lowe

I think the [snook] population was doing very well 'til we had this freeze [1981]. This freeze, they tell me, killed a lot of them...froze them to death.

Nellie Coleman

I remember three times when it froze enough to kill fish over there [on Cayo Costa].

I remember some winter kills on Cayo Costa when I was young. We picked up lots of snook [that were paralyzed from the cold water] to eat.

In those days... that was the only time you could get a snook, when he was half froze. Otherwise, you couldn't hold him in the net. He would bust it [the old fiber nets].

Esperanza Woodring

It freezes a few of them, but I do not think that is as bad as the red tide. Of course, we had a freeze in December, and there was a lot of fish along the beach here. Ralph [Woodring, her son] scooped up a bunch of mullet. He kept a whole bunch of mullet that were frozen [for bait].

Mary "Mamie" Weeks

[After the freeze] they went out the next day and went up these creeks. There were holes where the fish would be frozen and they took their dip nets and got them [for the fish house or to eat].

Red Tide

Red tide is a marine phenomenon that occurs commonly in subtropical waters. It is caused by an over-abundant bloom of plant-like phytoplankton called dinoflagellates. Their pigment causes the water to appear reddish. One kind of red tide, caused by the microorganism *Gymnodinium breve*, is common to Florida's west coast. The bloom kills fish, makes shellfish poisonous to eat, and causes respiratory discomfort to some people.

Much of the original research on red tide was compiled in the Charlotte Harbor area (Estevez et al. 1984:R58). Extensive studies, including the hypotheses on its stimuli and development, originated there. An article in the *Gasparilla Gazette* (April 1948, p. 3) said there would be a solution to the problem in three years. The red tide, first recorded in Charlotte Harbor in 1916, has occurred more frequently since 1946 (Estevez et al. 1984:R61). No early historic documents or archaeological data are available on the phenomenon. Oral histories are our only link to the effects of red tide on the precolumbian fisherfolk.

Red tide could have affected the available marine resource for the aboriginal inhabitants. It could have provided an easy short-term opportunity to collect a surplus of fish that were weak, dying, and floundering on the surface. The dinoflagellates release a toxin that paralyzes the fishes' gills, eventually suffocating them. The flesh, however, remains non-toxic. Fish could have been gathered in massive quantities and preserved to carry people through the catastrophe. On the other hand, shellfish survive the red tide but are rendered poisonous and inedible for some time after, even if cooked.

I asked my informants about red tide: when had they first seen it and how had it affected them.

Red-tide kill on Gasparilla Island, 1982. (Photo by Bob Edic.)

Tom Parkinson

People just cannot believe it. All I can tell you about is this area here, Charlotte Harbor. But the first red tide that I can remember was in 1947. Now, my father said they had it in 1916. But in 1947 it wiped the grouper out. It just wiped them out, and they are just now [1990] beginning to come back—offshore, too. I had boats going every day [from the fishhouse], and they were catching anywhere from a thousand to twenty-five hundred [pounds of grouper]. I think old Sam Whidden got twenty-five hundred [pounds] one day—that was about the biggest catch. They did that every day. When that red tide hit, they just all quit [fishing]. It was fifteen years, I reckon, nobody wanted to even go grouper fishing, because they were gone. There were not any. They are just coming back [now]. There is no reason why they did not have the same things back then [long ago].

Bill Hunter

Yes, there was [red tides] before the 1940s. Do not let anyone tell you that there weren't any. We had a storm here in 1919. We did not have one in 1920, but in 1921 we had the worst storm we ever had. But in 1920 there were all kinds of [dead] fish of every description. Then the red tide came in here. I walked down there on the beach, and it looked like, as far as you could see, the shrimp were just jumping out of the water. Whenever we went ashore, there were fish, shrimp, and all kinds of everything. There were big shrimp like that, that big around [jumbo size], all up and down that coast. You could see it [the red tide] coming in, laying in the dirt [on the beach].

We did not have any more of that [again] until 1945, when we had the same kind of thing. I did not eat any of the fish that time either, but there were a lot of people that picked up washtubs-full. I was scared to eat them, but at that time I did not know anything about it. It came during the time when most of the tourists came, but it was not like it is now. But there were a few people here that got washtubs full [of shrimp], pulled the heads off, put them in their frying pans, and cooked them and ate them. I watched them, but if you waited two or three days before you caught them, you were too late. They were all gone. All of the shrimp rotted and were gone.

The crabs crawled out of the water. They lay that way for a long time. The only houses there [on Gilchrist Avenue in Boca Grande] then were the ["Hal"] Hascal's and old [Henry] DuPont's and the widow [Louise] Crowninshield, places like that. But there was just a lot of fish. I have never seen so many [dead] fish in my life.

Alfonso Darna

In this area [it happened] when I was just a kid. I do not know what year it was [probably 1917-1918 (R.F.E.)]. Then the next I remember was in 1947. It killed millions of scallops by those islands [in Pine Island Sound]. Man, there were all kinds of scallops in there. You did not even have to get overboard to get them. You could just dip them up with a dip net. Just a few came back, but nothing like that. That was in 1947. That red tide was the worst I have ever seen. The fish were that high [knee deep] all along the beaches—on these island beaches—piled up dead. All types of fish! Stone crabs and everything else. That was a bad, bad time. A lot of people in 1947 ate these oysters, and a lot of them got sick from them. I mean bad sick, too! [They] had to go to the doctor.

When I was a kid, they called it the "poison water." They did not know what it was, they just called it the "poison water," and it killed tons of fish. They did not know too much about it then. I was not over eight or ten years old. I can just remember it. I saw all of these dead fish floating. Pelican Bay [on Cayo Costa] was just white with dead fish. Fishermen did not seem to know what it was. In fact, they had a boat that was stationed between Placida and Englewood. They would go out and take samples of the water and study it. I do not know what happened; they gave up on it. [They] could not do anything with it, I guess. But I am glad that we have not had any lately.

Richard Coleman

Things like red tide are hard on any kind of shellfish—clams, scallops, or oysters. Red tide works on them.

We did pretty good at it [grouper fishing]. There was a lot of grouper out there then. I believe it was about 1948 when it first hit—the red tide. The red tide killed most of them. It settled on those rocks and killed them.

Louis Darna says he has heard of a red tide way back then. But I think that was just a freeze, and it froze a lot of fish. That is the first that I remember [1948]. Boy, when that one hit, that was something. I had the *Faithful* then, and I would go out in this bayou [Boca Grande], and dead fish would just plow off of both sides of the boat. Millions of pounds. It was unbelievable. Bottom fish, catfish, sharks, everything. [They were] all along the boat. I had to run slow so that I would not bump them too hard.

The first time it happened I do not think anyone would eat them. They were scared of them. I know one time when the shrimp got on the beach they were still alive, jumping around on the beach. People went out there and got a whole bucket full of them. It did not hurt them.

Raymond Lowe, Sr.

We've had more red tide since the Second World War. Surely we did [have it] before the war, but I don't remember any. We've had it pretty regular here since the war. I understand in the paper yesterday they have red tide up in Longboat Key now [1990]. It didn't say anything about it today, but it usually moves down this way. That's what I can't understand about red tide—is why that certain areas have it, and they don't have it anywhere else. That's something I don't understand. We got two or three big rivers emptying into the Gulf down here as well. I don't think they know much at all about it at all. The first sign of that was the First World War, as far as I know. My father, he was telling me about it, it was real bad. Apparently after that, for many years, they didn't have any. That's another thing I

don't understand. I tasted some of that one time, I put it on my tongue, me and a friend of mine when we were kids. He said, "Let's taste some of that," and I said, "All right." We found a wad of it, as red as that curtain there, just a big glob of it, and we went right in the middle of it. Jesus Christ, it taste like a green persimmon. We didn't swallow any, just put it on our tongues.

During the war [World War II] they caught lots of grouper there [in Boca Grande Pass], three cent a pound! They claim the red tide swept through there and killed everything, but they are making a comeback [now].

Nellie Coleman

The only time I became acquainted with it [red tide] was when it started in here, in the '40s. But I did hear about it from some of the older people [that they had it back then].

Esperanza Woodring

I cannot remember the year, but it was after I had moved here [Sanibel Island]. I imagine it was about forty years ago—the worst one we ever had was the first one that I ever saw. All along those woods there [near her house on Woodring Point], when the tide was low, you could see these red things up in the mangroves. It looked like flowers. It was the mullets' roe, the red roe where the mullet had drifted up there and died, and the roe was still there. Roe is tough. It lasts a long time before it is spoiled.

They used to call red tide "poison water." I remember one time, and I did not know what it was all about. I had bought some nice big shiners, and I had them in my [bait] well. They were catching a lot of trout up there, you know. I looked down in the [bait] well, and my bait was doing this [quivering]. I said, "I wonder what in the world is the matter?" So I got a bucket and dipped some water out of the bay and put it in there, and, you know, they all went down to the bottom, dead as a door nail. I could not figure out what had hap-

pened. I was so disappointed and so mad. I went to the fish house over at St. James, and I got some ice. I went on up there fishing, and there were two or three boats up there. They were fishing, too. They had dead bait, [too], I guess. Anyhow, one of these guys said, "What kind of bait you got?" I said, "I got dead shiners." He said, "So have I." He said, "What happened?" I said, "I do not know. I had some beautiful bait, and all of a sudden they were down in the bottom of the boat." He said, "You know why I think it is?" I said, "No. I have no idea." He said, "It is that damn poisoned water." I said, "Sure enough." He said, "Yes. It is all over the bay. Same happened to me. I got up before daylight this morning. I caught my bait. I had the lid on the well, and by the time I got out to where I wanted to fish, every one of them was dead." I said, "Well, I iced mine." He said, "Well, they might bite those. I do not know. But I have not had a bite with dead shiners."

We had some [red tide] last year around Captiva [Island]. [It was] in the Gulf, but it did not come inside. Some of the dead fish floated in, but I do not think we got any of the [red] tide inside.

Well, these scientists, they are so smart, and they can figure out everything, but I do not think they know yet what causes all of that. They think they do, and they tell you what they think it is. I do not think they can do anything about it, because it is such a great big, tremendous area. How are you going to protect all of that stuff?

I think that it is something that grows in the water—some kind of algae or something. I do not know just what it is. They claim that it is in the water all the time, but in certain times it gets so thick that it starts killing the fish. The water is not poison. It is just the stuff that gets in the fish's gills.

I know about three years ago my sister and I went up there to one of these creeks. We were going to go fishing, and we found this net fisherman out there. He said, "Are y'all looking for fish?" We said, "Yes." He said, "Well, go over there and look on the bottom, and you can find all you want." My sister said, "Well, who wants dead fish?" "The red tide hit along that cove there, and a school of trout [got caught]. They are good." I said, "Well, why do you not jump overboard and dive them up?" He said: "Oh, no. I do not think I want to do that. So we had a dip net, and we went over there, and, sure enough, there were trout about like that [18 inches]. There must have been a whole school of them that were running from the [red tide]. We had a dip net, and we caught several that were already dying. They would come to the top, and we would dip them. We almost fell overboard. The water was about that deep [waist high]. I do not know why we did not get overboard and pick them up in our hands. Well, I do not think they will hurt you. That is what they say, but I would not want to eat one. But these fish were in good shape. You can tell a fish if he is bad by his gills. If it is black, leave it alone. But if it is red, it is okay. So we picked the fish up and looked at the gills. If it was all right, we put him in the boat; if it was a little bit tainted, we did not fool with it, and we threw it overboard." [The good ones were sold to the fish house.]

Bo Smith

[When I grouper fished] I had just been married a little while. I built that house on the bayou up there [in Boca Grande]..... that is when I lost it. We were struck with that red tide. I guess that was

during the war. The red tide wiped us out! There were so many dead fish floating that it was like plowing in a field...after that first red tide we had. You just cannot believe the fish [that were floating]. It was just like getting out there and plowing with a mule. You would be running in there and just plowing the fish aside. There were just millions of them. Just as far offshore as you would go, you would be in them. It was all up and down [the coast] pretty much. The [grouper] really have not ever come back like they were, unless you go way offshore.

Mary "Mamie" Weeks

[The first red tide that hit here] That was quite a few years ago. We don't have as much of it now as we used to. The first one I remember was right after the war, World War II, somewhere in that vicinity. That was our worst of it. It wasn't too bad here [in Estero Bay], but over on the beach they [the dead fish] piled up there.

Hurricanes and Storms

Hurricanes and storms can radically change fishing conditions instantly. Some extreme storms breach or fill in passes, deposit sand over grass flats and shoals, and form new land areas. Storms also flush the estuarine system, providing a natural cleansing of the shallow bays and salt marshes.

Some aboriginal sites were located in areas that are now passes between the barrier islands. Some, such as a site on the north side of Captiva Pass, have eroded, leaving just remnants of the former sites scattered on the beaches. Native American sites are also located by passes that have filled in, such as on Cayo Costa at Murdock Bayou (Herwitz 1977:71) and Gasparilla Island at the narrows about mid-island. Refuse in these sites indicates the use of both Gulf and estuary resources. Sites appear to have been abandoned when passes no longer provided easy access between the Gulf and bay. Data from these sites could be used to date the opening and closing of the passes. Blind Pass, between Sanibel and Captiva Islands, shows the dynamics of a pass in limbo (Harvey 1979:46-48), migrating as sands from the Gulf change it with every storm.

Geological evidence documented in core samples and C-14 dates indicate that a devastating hurricane hit the Calusa domain around 1710 (Davis et al. 1989). If accurate, this could have contributed to the demise of the Calusa. They had been displaced from their homelands and were in the Florida Keys by 1711 (Hann 1991:325-33). The combination of this "thousand-year storm" and slave raids by the Yamassee Indians from present-day South Carolina (Parks 1985:52-55) could have been the final blow that caused their downfall.

Data now being gathered on sea level fluctuations in the domain of the Calusa indicate that there have been significant rises and drops in the shallow estuarine environment through time (Stapor et al. 1991; Walker 1992; Walker et al. 1994).

Platt Pass [locally called Murdock Cut] on Cayo Costa was breached during the "No Name" storm of June, 1982 and again in March, 1993, during the "Storm of the Century." Both times I traversed the pass from bay to Gulf in a small boat. It provided a short, safe route to the Gulf at mid-point on Cayo Costa. Within a few days in both cases, although the Gulf side sanded in, the pass still provided an easy portage for a small boat over the beach to the Gulf. An archaeological site located at Murdock Bayou on the northeast side of Platt Pass indicates that this pass was open or was a portage in precolumbian times.

The historical fisherfolk had to deal with similar natural forces. A turn-of-twentieth-century (1900s)

Hurricanes

To adapt a phrase from Gentry, any study of the Charlotte Harbor Region entitled "A Review of Scientific Literature" would be incomplete without consideration of hurricanes. According to Bruun et al., "hurricanes are tropical cyclones with winds of 75 mph or more. A hurricane is characterized by a low pressure center with a counter-clockwise wind circulation (in the Northern Hemisphere) concentrated toward the center. As it moves along an undetermined track, the whole storm system is being continuously modified in shape, intensity, and direction by internal pressures and conditions."

A total of 64 tropical disturbances were recorded from 1830 to 1900, whereas 88 occurred from 1900 until 1955, over or near Florida. Since 1900, "a total of 30 known hurricanes and tropical disturbances have passed within a 50-mile radius of the study area."

Most sources agree that the strike frequency for hurricanes in the Charlotte Harbor area is on the order of 5 percent. Bruun et al. reported that the frequency of all hurricanes showed a marked change from one per year in the period 1900-1925 to two per year in the period 1925-1950. Within a strike year, the period in which hurricanes occur extends from May to December; September, October, and August are the peak months of occurrence, in that order.

Most hurricane damage is caused by tidal flooding, although rainfall, wind, and waves compound damage. Listed below are comments by the Army Corps of Engineers on locally important hurricanes:

Hurricane Of October 21-31, 1921

That storm was considered one of the most severe to strike the Gulf coast. It originated in the Caribbean Sea, followed a northerly path, and entered Florida about 115 miles north of the study area. Maximum flood elevations in the vicinity of Charlotte County were reported 7 to 11 feet above normal. High water elevations at Punta Gorda were about 8 feet.

Hurricane Of September 6-22, 1926

One of the most destructive of this century, the storm passed north of Puerto Rico and entered Florida at Miami. Causing great property damage, it entered the Gulf of Mexico at Ft. Myers. Waves of 11 to 12 feet were reported at Punta Rassa Point and over Sanibel and Captiva Islands.

Hurricane Of September 1-8, 1935

That hurricane was first observed east of Turks Island in the Bahamas and traveling toward the Florida Straits. It was one of the most severe tropical storms ever recorded. It passed over the Florida Keys taking a heavy toll of human life and property before proceeding up the west coast of Florida. Fort Myers Beach was flooded several feet deep. Wave heights were estimated at 16 feet.

Hurricane Of October 13-21, 1944

Originating in the western Caribbean, that storm entered the west coast of Florida about 40 miles north of Lee County. At Sanibel Island, winds of 100 miles an hour and 6-foot tides were reported by the United States Coast Guard. Tides and waves swept over the island, destroying many houses, wharves, and a ferry slip. A tide of 7 feet overtopped Gasparilla Island. Beaches on the Gulf side of the island were eroded landward as much as 50 to 60 feet in places.

Hurricane Of October 7-9, 1946

That hurricane formed in the northwestern Caribbean Sea and moved north-northeastward in the Gulf of Mexico, passed about 40 miles west of Lee County, and entered Florida in the Tampa Bay area. Much of Sanibel Island was inundated to depths of 1.5 to 3 feet. Maximum tides were about 4 to 5 feet on the lower Gulf coast.

(Excerpted from Estevez et al. 1984, pp. R34-R39.

farming settlement on Buck Key was wiped out in 1921 and 1926 by hurricanes and was never resettled (Marquardt 1992a:33). This process has no doubt repeated itself many times throughout the long history of Charlotte Harbor's occupation.

Nellie Coleman

Even if there's a storm when they [fish] are in the area, a lot of times they'll go past here, and you won't see them 'til the next spring or fall. They go from one place to another. If there's a storm up north of us here, they'll come back down here. You can tell, when a storm or something comes...those fish are [out of here]. By the time it's over with, there's nothing here...you have to wait awhile for them to come back. They go outside [to the Gulf], and they migrate also. In the fall of the year when they get back, they are all spawned 'cause they went somewhere else to spawn.

Bill Hunter

I used to fish Redfish Pass [between Captiva and North Captiva islands] when it opened up [after the 1926 hurricane]. I probably caught the first redfish ever caught out of Redfish Pass. I caught as high as 1,800 to 2,000 pounds a day out of that pass.

Mary "Mamie" Weeks

We had some pretty bad ones, but [Hurricane] Donna [1960] was the worst one. We were living in that big house there [pointing to the Week's family house.] It is on stilts about six foot above the ground. We stayed [there] and a lot of the people that lived here [at Weeks' Fish Camp and nearby] came and stayed in the house with my husband and I. When Donna went through [the Estero Bay area], the water was over their houses [on the ground]. When it [the storm] was over we had to go out. We had no water, no food, no electric.

[The water came up] right to the bottom of that big house there. You could go in that house, but it was right up to the floor...about six foot I imagine.

A school of mullet gather in
a "pod" preparing to leave the
estuary to spawn in the Gulf.
(Photo courtesy of Eunice Albritton).

CHAPTER 7

Fish

Mullet

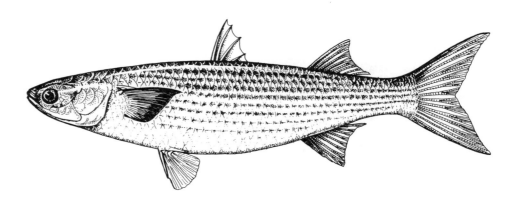

Mullet is a schooling marine fish found worldwide in shallow tropical and temperate waters. Torpedo-shaped and green-blue-silver in color, a mullet can grow to a length of three feet (91.4 cm) and weigh as much as 15 pounds (6.8 kg). The mullet family Mugilidae includes 100 species worldwide of which at least two (black and silver) are found in Florida waters, including Charlotte Harbor. *Mugil cephalus*, called locally black mullet, are commercially harvested in Charlotte Harbor today and were an important source of protein to Native Americans.

Black Mullet (also known as Striped Mullet)— Mugil cephalus
Description: color bluish-gray or green above, shading to silver on sides, with indistinct horizontal black barrings, white below; blunt nose and small mouth.
Where Found: inshore
Size: roe mullet common to three pounds, but in aquariums known to reach twelve pounds or more.
Remarks: adults migrate offshore in large schools to spawn; juveniles migrate inshore at about one inch in size, moving far up tidal creeks; frequent leapers; feed on algae, detritus, and other tiny marine forms. [Drawing by Merald Clark after Fishing Lines: Angler's Guide to Florida Marine Resources, *n.d.]*

The life cycle of the black mullet (*Mugil cephalus*) and the silver mullet (*Mugil curema*) begins and ends in the estuary. Black mullet leave the estuaries in late fall and early winter to spawn. When strong cold fronts move through the area in the fall, mullet gather in huge schools (called "pods" by local fisherfolk), migrating offshore through the passes to spawn in the Gulf of Mexico. Before the net ban (1995), they were caught in large numbers by commercial fishers. Silver mullet spawn in February or March in the Gulf and are also caught commercially, but in fewer numbers. Juveniles and adults of both species return to the estuaries to mature and complete the cycle of migration.

The Spanish-Cuban mullet fisheries of the 1700s exploited this vast resource, but emerging archaeological data suggest that the significance of mullet for the precolumbian cultures of Charlotte Harbor was not as great as would be expected given the significance of this resource to the modern fishery. This could be due to many factors. Mullet may be more tolerant of declining water quality and have proliferated while their predators have declined. The mullet population may be cyclical; there may not

have been as many mullet in precolumbian times. Preservation of mullet bones in the mounds may be limited because of processing techniques or trade. In historic times on Cayo Costa mullet were split, salted, and shipped out whole. Finally, mullet could have been rendered for oil by boiling, causing poor preservation of the bone.

Mullet have been harvested continually and still remained a major commercial industry until the net ban in 1995. The center of the United States commercial mullet fishery was the Charlotte Harbor area, which produced over 24 million pounds annually (Comp and Seaman 1985:386). The red roe of the larger female mullet is considered a delicacy and commands high prices on the world market.

Mullet was the single most important commercial species to the Charlotte Harbor fisherfolk. Many regard the mullet as their food fish of choice (Edic 1990). Mullet is of little interest to the sport-fishing industry, since it does not take a baited hook readily. The quantity taken by cast nets and snatch hooks by the recreational fishery is not known. Some mullet are used for cut bait by the sport and commercial fishing industries, but this is usually silver mullet.

The rendering of mullet oil by precolumbian cultures should be considered. Rolls of fat that form in the visceral cavity before and after spawning could have provided a valuable commodity similar to the eulachon oil used by the northwest coast Indians (Stewart 1982:149). I have rendered this oil and found it to be of high quality. It can be used for light, heat, and cooking, and it has high nutritional value. Some mullet oil rendered by boiling in 1982 is still in excellent condition in 1995. It is likely that native peoples prepared this useful product.

Tom Parkinson

They would strike bunches [of mullet in the fall with stop nets] and would get two or three hundred thousand [pounds]. ...Even an old fisherman that has caught as many as Fonso Darna talks about them being scarce [now]. I said, "What do you mean they are scarce?" He said, "Well, I remember we used to catch thirty, forty thousand [pounds] at a time [with a seine net]; now if you get a strike, and you get six or eight thousand [pounds], that is a real big strike." I said, "Yes, now you stop to think about that thirty or forty thousand that you caught. If

you had used a four and one-half or four and a quarter-inch [gill] net like you do now, you will not catch nothing but the red roe [the larger, female mullet]," I says, "How many would you have caught [in those days if you had used a gill net instead of a seine net]?" He says, "We probably would not have caught five thousand." [laughter]

You take a skinny mullet. It is a lot better eating than one that is full of roe. I used to kid Fonso [Darna] about it all the time. He was eating plenty [of mullet]. I would ask him, "Who wants to eat an old pregnant mullet?" [laughter] Well, to tell you the truth, I think the Indians would have known it.

[During roe season, mullet flesh becomes soft and oily. After spawning, mullet are emaciated from the ordeal. But soon they begin to fatten again and the flesh becomes firm and lean. It is then that they are considered the best eating by local fisherfolk.]

Mullet availability fluctuates through the years. I remember times fishing with my father when you could hardly catch a mullet. When abundant, prices are low;

when scarce, prices are high. The red tide killed a lot of mullet.

My theory, which is just as good as anybody's guess, would be that there was not as many mullet back in those days [precolumbian times]. Of course, people will argue the point with you. Because before they had all of these canals and stuff dug in the bay for them to get in and bunch up, they would all go out the passes [to spawn].

Bill Hunter

Mullet was the most important [fish to me]. I want you to know there were some mullet [here then]. But there were a lot of mullet that got caught and were on the black market. We were not allowed to catch them, because it was a closed season. I believe it was the first of November [they closed it]. Then they opened it up the fifteenth of January. Two and a half months they were closed.

Alfonso Darna

March, April, and May are no good for mullet. The mullet are all spawned out, and you were not getting much for them, what few mullet there are. Most of the fishermen went for mackerel and pompano at that time of year. The money that they made in the fall was off of mullet. I have always been strictly a mullet fisherman. That is all I ever fished for. Oh, I have fished for pompano and mackerel, but mullet is all you need. It has always been mullet fishing [for me].

Whatever I wanted [I kept to eat]. We mostly ate mullet, more than anything else. [My favorite food] would have to be a mullet. Pompano is good, but it seems like you get tired of pompano pretty quick.

In roe season we would fish out on the pass in the Gulf. Then in the summertime it would be all in the bay. We used pole skiffs for mullet in those days. We would tow [them] out with the big boat with an inboard. We towed out two or three skiffs—that all depended on how many were in the crew—then when you see mullet jumping, you anchor your big boat and get out and strike with your skiff. We poled the nets out in about eighteen-foot skiffs. They are really quieter. You could not strike out there in the middle with one net very well, because the fish would out-run you. If you had two boats, you could let go. Like this, would be the school [he demonstrates]; you would cross the let-go and take them in that way. Or [with] three [boats], there would be two here and one here. These two would let go and that one would go there, and one would meet him and this other one would cross to this net. That way you could take them in easy. You would put rubber on the back of your stern with the lead so it would not make so much noise, because that [lead line hitting the boat] would scare them. With that lead pounding on that stern, man, they would take off.

I did not start mullet fishing until I was about twenty years old. I went out once in a while with the older fellows, but I did not run my own crew until I was about twenty. That is when I first got my boat.

I start in August [mullet] fishing with a $7/8$ [3¾" gill net]. You know, you went with me a couple of times. I do not use anything

---

*Ruby Darna's Cornbread
(courtesy of Lana Engquist)*

Preheat oven 400°.

Grease cast iron skillet.

Mix together:

¾ cup flour

¾ cup cornmeal

3 teaspoons baking soda

2 pinches salt

2 pinches baking powder

Beat together:

1 cup buttermilk

2 eggs

Stir dry mix and batter together.

Pour off excess grease into batter.

Pour batter into skillet.

Bake 20 to 25 minutes.

---

smaller, because I do not gill net when the fish are small. You take the fishermen now. They are using about a 3-inch [stretch mesh] [or a] 3⅛-inch [stretch mesh]. I think most of them use a 3-inch, now. That is too small. They ought not to allow them to fish

Tom's Fish House Chowder
(courtesy of Mary Parkinson)

Cube potatoes. Chop green pepper (small amount). Salt. Cover with water and boil 'til tender. Boil it down pretty low.

Slice white bacon and remove rind. Chop or cube in small pieces. Brown in frying pan. Remove bacon parts and put in with potatoes and pepper.

Brown 1 chopped onion in bacon fat. Then put onion and all in pot with potatoes. Add butter to taste, about 1 tablespoon or maybe a little more.

Cube fish meat and add to pot and boil 'til done. 'Course you use black pepper to taste.

When you think all ingredients are done, add milk, part canned and part fresh, and heat to boil and remove from heat. Ready to serve.

Punta Blanca Fish House, circa 1928 (looking south). (Photo courtesy of Nellie Coleman.) This fish house and several others were destroyed by fire shortly after the net ban took effect in July, 1995.

with that small of a net. That is absolutely too little. But, that is the law, [or] I think that is the new law. For awhile there they were using 2¾-[inch stretch mesh], I think. I think [with] this new law, 3-inch is as small as you can use. But it takes so many of those mullet to weigh a hundred pounds. They do not pay anything for them, and then it kills so many little mullet. Then in a year's time [or] a couple of years, at least, they would be two-pound mullet [that] you could catch in a 4⅛-[inch] net.

You take a pompano or a mackerel, and you run this monofilament net right straight offshore, and fish will just go right on into it and hang up in it. With pompano, that is what we do with what we call a wing-ding net. We run it out there, and the pompano gill in it. But you take a mullet, he will never gill in it. No sir! He does not care whether it is monofilament or what it is. Now a lot of those fish do not learn like a mullet...they call him a "popeye" anyway. [laughter]

There's not as many silver mullet around as there used to be. In Bokeelia they

do a lot of silver mullet fishing. In fact, the silver mullet is in the fat season now [February]. They will have roe [spawn] in March and April. That is their season to spawn.

Richard Coleman

There are not many roe fish left. These mullet were raised up these rivers and canals and places like that. They stopped the commercial fishermen from going up there. You cannot fish up

Albert Lowe (Raymond's brother) with catch of large mullet at Gasparilla Village, circa 1930. (Photo courtesy of Boca Beacon.)

these canals anymore. All of these canals have houses all along there. These people have these cast nets, and, soon as the sun goes down, [they go down] there with their cast nets and catch themselves three or four mullet. The others up there will do the same thing. They all do that, and it ends up to be a whole lot of fish. You do not catch them because it is at night, and it is pretty hard to catch them. How are you going to catch them? It is all right to use cast nets—but you cannot use a mullet net up there!

Raymond Lowe, Sr.

I don't think there is as many mullet as there used to be, but, on the same token, we got so much traffic on the bay all the time, and the fish can't gather up like they used to. Back in the old days we had a two-month closed season, and it would give the fish time to gather up. When I was a kid, I think it was the twentieth of November 'til twentieth of January. They haven't had a closed season in many years, before the Second World War, forty years [ago].

I know a mullet is pretty smart, but I don't think he could see that glass [monofilament] net in the water. Why that old 920 cotton, it looked like a fence hanging out there.

We fished a little bit in the fall of the year during run season [mullet season]. But as time went by, well, we devoted most of our fishing time to mullet fishing. Then this war came along [World War II], and things were getting pretty bad—that was in 1942.

We used three [different sizes of nets]. The inch and five-eighths, that be three and one-quarter-inch stretch [we started with in summer]. In the run season, a four-inch stretch. We never did use inch and one-half [3" stretch], but inch and five-eighths; that's three and one-quarter-inch stretch. And a six-eighth [3½"] and seven-eighth [3 ¾"], and a four-inch [stretch].

In June or so, when the mullet started getting over that run ordeal (spawning), [they] get fat. They started shaping up along about June, July, and August.

They [scientists] don't have a great deal of information on mullet. Why, I don't know, they track other fish. They [mullet] come in here just like birds; they are migratory. Where they go, we just don't know.

There used to be thousands and thousands of silver mullet, but you don't never see any of them anymore. We used to catch them; we had a real small mesh net. They weren't too much to eat or anything, but they did catch them. I don't think they got a hell of a lot for them; they only caught them in the spring of the year [when they were spawning].

Nellie Coleman

I guess in the old days they fished mostly for the mullet. They fished for them in roe season in the fall of the year. There's mullet around all year, but they're easy to catch in the fall during roe season when they get in big schools. But mullet, like all other fish, they're migratory. They go out through the pass and scatter; nobody knows where they go.

You think all the [Indians] had to do to catch a mullet was go out there at night and shine a light, and they'd just jump right in the boat. They'd jump right in the boat! But I suppose they had some kind of nets [too].

Esperanza Woodring

Mullet was [the] most important species [to us]. Probably [because] they were easier caught in the nets. I do not know if there were more of them, but I presume there were.

When the mullet were running, they would be the easiest because they would be in these schools. Now, you are not going to believe this, but they used to come along the edge of that beach there, and the porpoise and big fish would be [in] just schools and schools. My husband Sam used to go out there with a pitchfork. Now, you are not going to believe that, [but] he would catch whatever he wanted to eat the next day with a pitchfork. They would be right up there. I imagine you could have picked them up with your hand because they were so close to the beach. You see, they were running from these other big fish that were on the outside. Every now and then they would get in there and get them a mouthful of whatever they wanted, and the poor old mullet were trying to get away from them. They were right up [close to the beach], most especially on moonlight nights. You could just see them, you know.

Down there at the [Sanibel] lighthouse, they used to have a big, long dock out there. They used to go out there with snatch hooks. Do you know what a snatch hook is? [A snatch hook is generally a large weighted treble hook. It is dropped in the water and "snatched" quickly in order that it might snag into a passing fish.] They would just snatch them. They would tear the poor mullet up. You would see the roe streaming down. Well, they stopped that now. You cannot do that anymore. Down there at Blind Pass, across that bridge, they said it would be ridiculous the way they would slaughter the poor mullet. You know, they would just hook it enough that he would flop off, and the roe would be scattered all over. No doubt some of the fish died, I imagine.

You can take a fisherman, and he has got all kinds of fish in his boat. If he is going to eat well once in a while he might change, but most of the time what do you think he would take home to eat? Mullet.

Bo Smith

I used to mostly seine fish. That is where you strike on the beach and pull them ashore. Then you just bail them in the boat. The net was about [one] inch, inch and a half [stretch], something like that. If you had a bigger net, you could gill it full, and you could not handle them. You have to have it small enough [mesh] so they would not gill. That way you could just bring them upside the boat, bail your boat full, and bring another boat up and bail it full.

I have done quite a bit of gill netting, but it was so much easier with that seine. Of course, gill netting, I guess, you could always catch a few fish every day. With a seine you might not get a catch but once a week, but you would catch twenty or thirty thousand [pounds] or something like that, you know. Maybe it would be two or three weeks before you catch anything. [And] you always had five or six men. You would think twenty or thirty thousand was a lot [of] fish, but, by time you split it between five and six people, it really was not that many.

We could sell every mullet we caught [to the Gasparilla Fishery]. They had box cars. They would weigh them and put them in them wheelbarrows and carry them in there and dump them in box cars with a sheet of ice. The whole car was just mullet on ice.

[By] Thanksgiving you would catch a few fish, you know. Or [at] Halloween you could catch a few. Then they would get in bigger bunches in November, December, and January. I usually quit and [would] go back to guiding the first of February.

I have done quite a bit of summer fishing [for mullet]. Old Woodrow Coleman and I each had a little boat. And then I started with Johnny Downing. We were using six-eighth [3.5" stretch mesh]. Then we would go to seven-eighth [3.75" stretch mesh]. If that fish does not fit that nylon net, he would go through it or get bounced off it.

A lot of people fished earlier for smaller fish with five-eighth nets [3.25" stretch mesh], but I never did. When I started, I just went with a six-eighth, then a seven-eighth, and then I went to a four-inch [stretch mesh]. They are using four and one-quarter inch [stretch mesh], so they can get mostly red roe mullet.

They talk about mullet being so scarce now. I have seen back then when you could not hardly catch any mullet. Now, of course, they get back in these keys in these little boats with kickers [small motors], you know. We could not do that [back then].

You always get them just ahead of a front. When I first started we were getting three and four cents [per pound], and then they jumped up to six and eight cents a pound. I think it was over Christmas [they had a closed season]. In that month, it was in roe season. I do [think the closed season did some good], because you could see bunches of mullet then, and now you do not see those big schools like that much. You would go to a pass, and you would see forty, fifty, sixty thousand pounds in a bunch.

What has helped these fishermen now, I think, is glass nets. It is just easier fishing [with a glass net]. With cotton nets, we had to wrap them up, close them up, and then drive them in the net. Sometimes we had to rope them down, you know. With glass nets, you just have to see which way they're going and strike them. Just run that thing out [and] around them. You do not even have to close it up. Just run it the way they are going.

I still think there are just as many fish as there ever were. You know, you think there are no fish. You go out two or three days, and you do not see any. All of a sudden you get a front, and I guess they come out of those rivers and creeks and cuts, and there will be bunches of fish.

Grady Sands

 When my dad first came to this country down in here, the only way they had of transporting fish [mullet] was to split and salt [them]. The only way they had of moving them was sailboat. They had one sailboat. My dad did sponge fishing up around Tarpon Springs [north of Tampa].

He was a skipper on a sponge boat up there for awhile. He fished for mullet [here]. All around these islands here [Bull and Turtle Bays]. Of course, fish were scarce at times, but back then, we had a closed season [on mullet]; run season from the fifteenth of December until the twentieth of January. That was the law. Of course, when they passed this deal on the snook [gave it game fish status], that is when they opened up the closed season [on mullet].

When I first started commercial fishing—that is, when I was first here—I fished with Old Man Sam Joiner [in the 1930s, early 1940s]. We caught fish, [and] I mean by the goddamn boat load. We were getting one cent a pound. I have caught them for less than that. They say not, but I know better.

We would stop-net Big Creek [also known as Whidden's Creek], but a lot of times we would cut it off just from down where the boat is there and go all the way across yonder. It was not just one net. We had nets tied together. [They were] cotton, but they were tar dipped to preserve them. It would go across Big Creek and then go down to the cut-off where it goes into Turtle Bay. I would cut that off. A lot of people do not know this—they do not realize it, but a mullet goes against the tide. They do not go with the tide. Trout, pompano, and stuff like that goes with the tide, but mullet goes against the tide. When you cut it off and that tide goes out, those fish go right back in that creek. Then all we do is go up there, cut it back off, and take the boat and pull it [the net] back down [the creek].

Grady's father, Eugene Sands Sr., ca. 1930s. (Photo courtesy of Eunice Albritton.)

I have drug that ... place over there so ... many times and this one over here [so many times] that it is pathetic.

I guess our biggest catch would run anywhere from twelve to fifteen thousand [pounds].

We never graded fish out. [Prior to ca. 1950, mullet were bought by weight only. After that time, the fisherfolk began grading them, separating the larger from the smaller fish. In the 1980s, they began grading them further, separating the largest red-roe mullet from smaller mullet.] When I first started, a red-roe mullet and a white-roe mullet was all the same. That was before the Japanese came in. [The Japanese prefer the red roe as a delicacy. Thus, red-roe mullet bring a higher price per pound.]

We did not even know what ice was [in the 1930s and 1940s]. [laughter] It makes a difference. We used to go leave Gasparilla [Village] over there like at 6:00 in the afternoon. We had the boat with an engine in it with three pole skiffs tied behind it. We would tow it to right out here in the bay, anchor that boat, then we would split up. My dad would go one way, I would go one way, and my uncle would go [one way]. We covered the islands [in the Bull Bay and Big Creek areas]. We would come back to the boat at daylight (or sun-up, whatever), tie on to it, and the fish [we caught were] still lying right there on the floor [of the boat]. [We would] carry them all the way to Gasparilla and get there at, say, 8:00 or 9:00 in the morning. [We would] unload them,

and they were just as hard and firm as if you had iced them at the time you put them in the boat. Well, that is your pollution [that makes them go bad now]. The only time we used ice back in the 1940s [was when we were] going grouper fishing. Now, we carry ice.

[Grady now describes how local fishermen at Placida struck a huge school of mullet that was leaving Gasparilla Sound and heading for Gasparilla Pass and the Gulf of Mexico in the fall of 1990. After first spotting the school, the fishermen had to wait a day because, beginning in 1990, mullet in the roe season were partially closed to fishing. Mullet were not allowed to be caught during weekends, from sundown on Fridays until sundown on Sundays.]

They [the mullet] came down the river up yonder out of Punta Gorda or wherever. But on Saturday night I was working there at the fish house [in Placida], before they caught these fish on Sunday night. I had went and gassed up the trucks, and I heard a porpoise right there in back of the fish house. I looked out there, and that whole flat out there was solid black with mullet. They [the porpoise] raised cane there awhile. Then they went on out to the mouth of the channel—it was either him or another one—and then over by that bird island [a bird rookery on a mangrove island near the mouth of Coral Creek] they were doing the same thing. So I walked down to the entrance of the creek there going into the marina. Up in that marina was the awfulest sight up there you have ever seen. Porpoises! They had to be in mullet. You could listen down that shoreline, and you could just hear them coming. I figured those fish never stopped until they got to that bridge. They went in there [the mouth of the creek] and then came back out. They went to that bridge and got together [in a huge pod]. And Mitchell Keene, I understand (now, do not quote me on this because I do not know) found it. He started following it [the pod], and they [the mullet] were going out in the pass, so he called Donnie. Well, Donnie came to him and saw what it was. He had a seine on his boat then. And he had a pocket that would hold approximately 30,000 pounds. He said, "Well, this pocket is too little." He went back to the house and got the other one, which had a pocket that would hold approximately 100,000 [pounds]. [After they netted them,] they pulled them so tight [that] they pulled the lead line in two. I know [they broke the lead line] once, and

I do not know how many more times. Well, Timmy Dixon (and I think his brother or some of them were the ones that put all of this in the newspaper [*Boca Beacon*] about it) had been following a bunch of fish besides that. They came on out, and he was waiting on them [the fish he was following] to get on down the beach. He looked, and he seen what was going on, so he did not strike them. They went right on and got in with the others that Mitchell and them were following. So when they struck, he hauled off and got over in the compass [within the larger seine net] and run his gill net in there. He got 8,600 [pounds of] nice [big red-roe] mullet. Well, now, had they done what they ought to have done...seeing what kind of a bunch of fish they were and called all the fishermen. There were enough fish there for everybody, they could have gone out there with those big-mesh nets and struck those fish, strained them out, [and] let the smaller-class fish go. That is what hurt us [taking the small fish and wasting them because they could not be sold]. Because if he was that long [big enough possibly to have red roe, or 8-10 inches long], we had to check to see if he had a red roe. That is ridiculous [because only a very few of the small fish have it].

All the holes are full when they pulled them [the nets] so tight. They said the lead line was about, I do not know how far away from the beach out there in a circle, and they were solid. You could walk on them from there to the beach. They got there and bailed them [removed mullet with a dip net] without ever pulling the lead line and shoring [beaching] them.

It is a once-in-a-lifetime experience, but actually they did not make nothing out of it. They made money, understand, but they did not make the money they would have made if they had done it like I am talking [about]. Everybody would have still got fish. And, of course, what got away would have probably went on north, which is the direction they generally go, or offshore.

I do not know about the good pounds [the mullet that were not too bruised or too small to sell]. They figured 172,000 [pounds] went through the fish house [at Placida] not counting what went other places. They loaded one boat and went back to Cortez [Manatee County], and the man turned them down because they were too small.

Elmer Johnson

In them days you didn't make much money. I fished [for mullet] many a night for a penny a pound. [I fished for mullet] in roe season. We done stop netting in the bays, gill netting, and used seines too. We used about two or three, we put out a thousand of yards of net. We use to catch them by the thousands you know, we used to "stop" big nets. I caught a hundred and ten thousand [pounds] in one stop. [I sold them to] the Punta Gorda Fish Company. And Chadwick Brothers, too. I fished all my life.

Mary "Mamie" Weeks

My husband was a commercial fisherman. Of course, our main fish was mullet.

Redfish

Redfish (*Sciaenops ocellatus*) have been important to local fisherfolk for many centuries. Redfish bones found in Charlotte Harbor's precolumbian shell mounds indicate that they represented an important food resource. My informants tell me that redfish are strong and destructive to natural-fiber nets. This suggests to archaeologists that

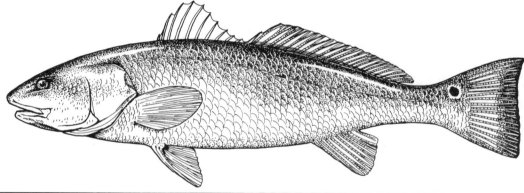

Redfish — Sciaenops ocellatus; *Family Sciaenidae, Drums*
Description: chin without barbels; copper-bronze body, lighter shade in clear waters; one to many spots at base of tail (rarely no spots); mouth horizontal and opening downward; scales large.
Where Found: inshore
Size: one of 27 inches weighs about 8 pounds.
Remarks: red drum are an inshore species until they attain roughly 30 inches (4 years), then migrate to join the nearshore population; spawning occurs from August to November in nearshore waters; sudden cold snaps may kill red drum in shallow, inshore waters; feeds on crustaceans, fish, and mollusks; longevity to 20 years or more. [Drawing by Merald Clark after Fishing Lines: Angler's Guide to Florida Marine Resources, *n.d.]*

spears, traps, or hook-and-line were used by the Calusa and their predecessors to capture this fish.

Cuban fishermen traded for and harvested redfish in the area by the early 1700s (Covington 1959:114-115). The rancho fishermen caught and traded them to Cuba during the 1800s when they could not supply mullet. They were easily caught with hook and hand line commercially when encountered in large schools during spawning. Later, strong nylon nets were used in their capture. There has always been a market for them though prices were low. They remained an important economic commodity to the commercial fisheries until they were given "gamefish status" in 1990. This prevented their commercial sale and limited the size and numbers that could be caught. Known as a strong and relentless fighting fish, they remain a popular gamefish today. Though not highly prized as a food fish by the senior fisherfolk I interviewed, they were occasionally eaten. Now with "Blackened Redfish" made popular by a famous Louisiana chef, they are in high demand by the restaurants around the country.

Bill Hunter

I probably caught the first redfish ever caught in Redfish Pass [when it opened up in the 1926 hurricane and breached Captiva Island, forming North Captiva and Captiva islands]. I caught [with hook and hand line] as high as eighteen hundred to two thousand pounds a day out of that pass. May, June, and July was all I fished there. I only fished the times they were there. I never ate redfish, cobia, shark. Stuff like that I do not eat.

Alfonso Darna

You know, fishermen never did catch very many redfish, [at least] not a long time ago when I was a kid. They did not have anything to catch them with unless they went to the Gulf on the beach [where] they could catch them with a seine. But the [gill] nets they used in those days were cotton nets, and they were weak. Those redfish would go right through them. They had 920 cotton [nets]. I was grown before fishermen actually started catching, [or] had nets to catch, redfish. [They used] that strong nylon trammel net, 336, I think, inside the net. [It was] nylon, and, boy, that is strong.

They had special nets for redfish. You cannot catch a redfish unless his gills will fit that mesh. You cannot catch that big old redfish with that old cotton net. He will just tear that all to pieces.

I do not care for [eating] redfish too much. In fact, I do not care for them at all.

Richard Coleman

A redfish would break [the cotton nets] pretty fast, too. You would catch one every now and then, but you would lose more than you catch.

You did not get much for them, but you could sell them. [I] hardly ever ate them.

Raymond Lowe, Sr.

We didn't eat many redfish and no snook at all. The spice kills the taste [when they're "blackened"].

Nellie Coleman

Redfish did [break our nets]; trout weren't so bad. They caught them on hook and line, anyway.

Esperanza Woodring

I do not think they fooled with redfish [on Cayo Costa], at least I know my grandfather did not. Now, my father did...he had a gill net. He used to mullet fish in season. Then when the season was over, he used to catch trout or redfish or whatever would sell at the market. He used to catch a lot of redfish in the nets.

We would go out there to catch a redfish to eat. He would catch one, and, if that did not suit him, why, he would throw him back overboard. He would fish until he caught the right size.

Bo Smith

I fished [for] redfish with hand lines. They broke the nets. If they ever got that gill in them smaller mesh nets, there ain't nothing would stop them. September is when they bunch up, and I used to catch them in my seine along the beach. I've eaten some, but they smell so bad when you're cleaning them; ... that's a stinking fish.

I fished redfish in Captiva Pass three or four times with hand lines. I caught quite a few of them, but that was hit-and-miss.

There are the most redfish that I have ever seen now. Everywhere you go there are redfish. I tell you, this thing [the size and limit law] really helped. When they cut it down to two redfish per person and a certain length, I really believe that helped. [The law is one fish eighteen inches or over, and none longer than twenty-seven inches per person, with no commercial sale of the species.]

Oh, yes, it really hurt [the fishermen economically]. I mean, they cannot catch any, you know. If you catch one in a net, you better turn him loose.

The commercial fishermen do not hurt them as badly as the sport fishermen. I mean, the sport fishermen get out there, and there are so many of them. If everybody catches two, that is a lot of redfish.

Grady Sands

 The redfish is coming back. Now, I was talking to Mitchell Keene some time ago, and he had been in the islands [Bull Bay] fishing one night. So I asked him, "How are spider crabs down there?" He said, "They cannot survive." I said, "What is the matter?" He said, "Them damn redfish are eating them up as fast as they hatch." [laughter] He said, "The redfish are out of this world." Yes, I would have to say that ban on [the commercial sale of] redfish is what is responsible [for bringing them back]. There are a lot of them. And snook, too.

The only way I netted [redfish] or anything like that [was when we fished with a stop net]. When they had the closed season on mullet, we stop-netted a lot of times.

[The old cotton gill nets] would hold a trout all right, and I guess if you could get a net big enough that would gill a redfish, you would catch a few. You did not catch too many until they went to nylon. The seine nets—the mesh was so small, they could not get their mouth in it. That mouth is what busts it.

There was a market for them, not nothing like there would be now. But redfish, there is just any amount of those things you want to look at, they tell me. If they do go and have this closed season on mullet [again], and they do not open it on redfish, these guys are going to be hurting, because that is what they did in that month and a half of closed season; they trout and redfished. And they caught a lot of trout. They did not catch that many redfish—maybe five or six hundred a night, or something like that—but they did not really try for redfish as much as they did trout, because, with trout, the price was a lot different.

Spotted Sea Trout

The bones of several species of sea trout are identified in the food assemblage of archaeological sites in Charlotte Harbor (Walker 1992:265-366), representing an important food resource that was available throughout the year. The spotted sea trout, like redfish, is a strong fish that can break through natural fiber nets but can easily be caught with hook and line. Large sea trout along with redfish may in part explain the presence of aboriginal hook-and-line fishing technology in addition to net fishing.

Trout was also caught by the early Cuban fishermen and they were commercially fished throughout the twentieth century. With the advent of nylon and monofilament gill nets in the 1940s, they could be easily caught. They provided a year-round alternative to mullet fishing because they are always available in the estuaries. Trout commanded a good price compared to other species. Caught in large numbers using hook and line, they were sold to the fisheries by recreational as well as commercial fisherfolk.

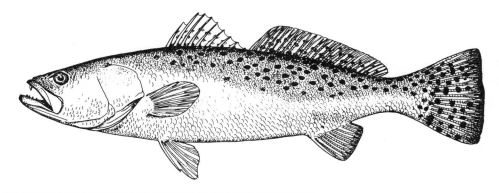

Spotted Sea Trout — Cynoscion nebulosus; *Family Sciaenidae, Drums*
Description: dark gray or green above, with sky-blue tinges shading to silvery and white below; numerous distinct round black spots on back, extending to the dorsal fins and tail; black margin on posterior of tail; no barbels; no scales on the soft dorsal fin; one or two prominent canine teeth usually present at tip of upper jaw.
Where Found: inshore and/or nearshore over grass, sand, and sandy mud bottoms
Size: common to 4 pounds on west coast, larger on east coast
Remarks: matures during first or second year and spawns inshore from March through November; often in association with seagrass beds; lives mainly in estuaries and moves only short distances; adults feed mainly on shrimp and small fish; prefers water temperatures between 58 and 81°F, and may be killed if trapped in shallow water during cold weather; longevity 8 to 10 years. [Drawing by Merald Clark after Fishing Lines: Angler's Guide to Florida Marine Resources, *n.d.*]

As their numbers declined during the 1980s, more regulations were put in place restricting size, limits, and sale. Fearing the loss of yet another economically important species, the commercial fishing interests fought legislation that would restrict their catch. Sport and commercial fishers each blamed the decrease in trout population on the other. This was the single greatest cause of the enmity between the sport fishermen and the commercial fishing industry. This confrontation would lead to a ban on net fishing in 1995.

Bill Hunter

You know trout seem to spawn all year around. I have caught a lot of trout during the summer. I used a hand line with two hooks on it and no lead or anything. You did not throw it out there but about here to there [ten feet]. You would get two trout by the time it hit the water. It was faster in a school of trout [than a pole]. I'd get a trout, pull him in, take him off, break his neck. If you did not break his neck, he would flop around and scare all of them off. If you find a good pothole where trout will hang out, about an hour or two before the tide finishes up [the last two hours of the low tide], you will catch the hell out of trout.

Richard Coleman

You would catch a few trout, but those old cotton nets would not hold a trout too much. I do not eat many trout. I did not care for them much.

Raymond Lowe, Sr.

I fished for trout along the beach in the summer and sold them. Trout can have roe in them anytime.

Nellie Coleman

Trout were caught with hook and line, because they broke the cotton nets. The trammel nets would catch them when they [the trammel nets] came out [in the 1940s]. They were our [my husband's and my] most important species fished for, because we fished them most of the time [all through the year]. We ate mostly trout 'cause that's what we fished for most of the time.

Bo Smith

I used to trout fish with a cane pole. I'd catch my bait at daylight in the morning with a little seine and catch sardines. I'd fish down the shore from Turtle Bay and Bull Bay. I'd catch anywhere from fifty, seventy-five to a hundred pounds a day. That's when the weather's good.

Small Food Fish

Pinfish (*Lagodon rhomboides*), pigfish (*Orthopristis chrysoptera*), and spot (*Leiostomus xanthurus*) are small fish that inhabit the shallow waters of the estuarine grass meadows.

These small fish represent a great portion of the food fish remains found at many archaeological sites in the Charlotte Harbor area (Walker 1992). Netting smaller fish for food may have been one way the aboriginal people protected their food sources from depletion; or they may have used small fish as a food source when nothing else was available. These small fish are the most abundant (Wang and Raney 1971) and perhaps among the hardiest (Storey and Gudger 1936) in the Charlotte Harbor area.

Tom Parkinson

I do not see where March would have been one of the hungriest months. The one fish you could always get is pinfish and that variety [small fish]. Pinfish and pigfish are good eating and available all year long. The red tide wipes them out first, but they are the first to stage a comeback too.

Nellie Coleman

Pinfish were eaten when times were tough. They were always available.

Esperanza Woodring

We caught pinfish and ate them when nothing else was available. We caught them in traps made from old pots. We saved the "spots" we caught in the nets and ate them ourselves. They are good pan-fried.

Net-mending party at Gasparilla Village, circa 1920. (Photo courtesy of Eunice Albritton.)

CHAPTER 8

Nets

Nets are essential technological implements to the fisherfolk of Charlotte Harbor today as they have been for thousands of years. Until the advent of nylon in the 1940s, natural fibers had been used for net cordage for thousands of years.

In the Charlotte Harbor area the precolumbian inhabitants left no written record of their net-fishing techniques, but net-fishing artifacts have been found at many of the archaeological sites in the area (Marquardt 1992b:212-214). Some net-mesh gauges found at the Useppa Island archaeological site date to ca. 3500 to 4800 years ago, during Archaic times (Marquardt 1995).

My interviews with the local senior fisherfolk convey the evolution of technology—netting from natural fibers such as cotton and flax to nylon and monofilament nets, from simple seine and gill nets to trawl and trammel nets of intricate designs; from pole skiffs to power boats; from locating fish from lookouts along the beach to aerial surveillance and electronic fish finders.

The strategy for net fishing is simply to capture fish by trapping them in some way. Stop nets can be used for traps to impound fish. Dip nets can be used to haul fish from the water with long poles. In open water a simple seine net with floats on the top and weights on the bottom can be used to encircle fish or pull them to shore for capture. A

relatively new invention is trawling, where a net is dragged over the bottom behind a boat. This also works well for shrimp, scallops, and other bottom dwellers. Cast nets can be used by one person and thrown over a small school of fish with weights that spread the net in a circle, sinking it to the bottom and allowing the fish to be hauled in.

The appropriate size mesh, depth, length, and strength of the net are important for targeting specific species of fish. Gill nets of specific sizes can be used to target certain species and sizes of fish by letting smaller fish pass through the mesh opening and deflecting larger ones around the net. Those of the chosen size are "gilled" by the net and held tightly until removed.

This net wheel was built by Gus Cole at Gasparilla Village. It was used to haul nets out of boats in order to lime and dry them, ca. 1930. (Photo courtesy of Janice Busby.)

Nets require constant maintenance. However, that has been minimized by knowledge gained through oral tradition, so that the nets are not torn up by fish too large or strong for the twine, chewed up from leaving the net in too long where crabs are present, or damaged from bottom snags. Meshes can also be broken by improperly removing fish. Net rot and rodent and insect damage also have to be dealt with, usually by spreading, drying, and treating the nets after use. Local aboriginal netting made from plant fiber would have been vulnerable to all of the above conditions.

Senior fisherfolk tell of using cotton and then flax nets before the advent of nylon and monofilament and attest to the maintenance required to protect the nets from damage. Preservation by tarring or liming fiber nets was a constant process, as was repair work to damaged mesh. We do not know what preservation materials were available to the aboriginal fisherfolk or how they dealt with the same problems.

Netting Materials

Palm fiber has been identified as the fiber used in aboriginal fish nets from Key Marco (Newsom 1989). Other types of natural fiber were no doubt also used. Robin Brown (1994:85-90) has demonstrated that strong and serviceable cord can be manufactured from several native plant species.

Cotton (*Gossypium*) was used in the nineteenth and first half of the twentieth century for net cordage.

Flax (*Linaceae usitatissimum*) is a natural fiber made from the flax plant. Soft cordage from flax was

Cabbage palm (Sabal palmetto) *fiber. (Photo courtesy of Robin Brown.)*

Twisting cordage, palm fiber. (Photo courtesy of Robin Brown.)

used around the turn of the twentieth century for making nets.

Nylon and monofilament nets introduced after the 1940s are much stronger and thinner than fi-

ber nets and require much less maintenance. Fish have difficulty seeing them. Because nylon and monofilament nets stretch more than fiber nets, these nets hold the fish more tightly. Fish such as trout

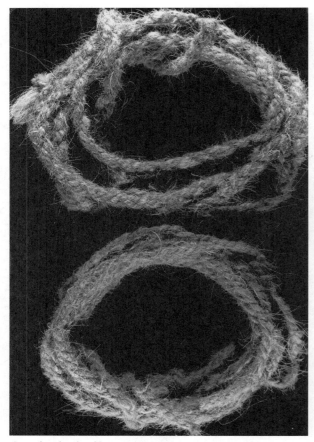

Completed palm fiber cordage. (Photo courtesy of Robin Brown.)

Different diameters of palm cordage. (Photo courtesy of Robin Brown.)

and redfish, which would have broken through the older netting material, can easily be caught. Many local senior fisherfolk consider the greater effectiveness of "glass" (monofilament) nets to be the biggest cause for the decline in species.

Unlike natural-fiber nets, nylon and monofilament do not easily biodegrade. When lost to swift currents or abandoned, they can have long-term devastating effects on marine life.

Once while skin diving on the old railroad

trestle that spans Gasparilla Pass, I observed a cast net that had been snagged on a piling for some time. It was in about ten feet of water. Trapped in the net were several dead mullet from the original catch. This had attracted many other scavengers that were now hopelessly entangled. These included other fish, crabs of several types, shrimp, and a diving bird.

Net Types

Twentieth-century fisherfolk of Charlotte Harbor have used a variety of nets. *Stop nets* were single-bunt, heavy-duty twine nets made from flax or cotton with floats and weights. (The bunt is the sagging part of a fish net.) These nets were preserved by being soaked in vats of hot tar. Fishermen could tie several stop nets together to block off an inlet. The small mesh size captured most fish by blocking their escape. The net forms a pocket, and, once trapped, fish are removed with the use of other nets. These nets can be set on the high tide and left until the tide is low. Catches of 200,000 pounds and up have been reported by informants. Because of this effectiveness and the consequent threat of overfishing, stop nets were outlawed in Florida in the 1930s.

Seine nets were single-bunt (1-2" stretch mesh), of lighter twine, and shorter in length than a stop net. Seines were usually pulled ashore, since there is no pocket. These nets were made of small-mesh (1-2") cotton twine in varying depths and lengths. Floats and weight lines are used.

> Net size can be expressed as a square mesh (the length of one side a mesh) or a "stretch" mesh (the length of the diamond stretched tight). A net mesh that is 1 ½" on a side is 3" "stretched."

From the "Goode" report (1844-1887):

The seine nets measure up to 480 feet and have depths of 24 feet. The seines above referred to, and varying considerably in size, require from four to twelve men each to handle them. The fishing is carried on from the middle of August to the middle of January, and the variety chiefly taken is mullet. Ten to twenty thousand fishes are frequently taken at a haul. More are often surrounded by the seine than can be hauled out. There is no bag or pocket to these seines, therefore they are hauled out on the beach.

Gill nets in Charlotte Harbor ranged from 3-4½"-stretch mesh and were used with floats and weight lines. Gill nets were released from a boat with a weighted line called a "let-go." These nets were generally used to strike fish that were visually spotted and were surrounded or cut off with the net. Specific-sized fish were caught by gilling in certain-sized mesh. Smaller fish passed through the mesh opening, and larger ones bounced off.

According to Goode (1844-1887:34), the gill net was introduced in the area around 1880 by "northern fishermen." It was not until the turn of the twentieth century that it gained popularity in Charlotte Harbor.

At first gill nets were used with sailing boats and "pole skiffs." The net was released into the water by quietly lowering the weighted end of the net, which was bundled up in the back of the boat. It was then slowly poled around the fish with a long oar, called a poling oar. With the advent of inboard motor skiffs around 1910, several pole skiffs could be towed to the fishing grounds. This allowed the fisherfolk to work in unison, cover more area, and return to the fishery more quickly to insure a fresh catch. These motor skiffs were later rigged for net fishing and used to "strike" the fish (encircle them with the net). These were all but replaced by the development of a fast shallow-draft boat known locally as a "kicker boat." An outboard

Net mesh gauges are used to maintain proper mesh size. These precolumbian artifacts fashioned from bone and shell were excavated by archaeologists in the Charlotte Harbor area. (Photo courtesy of FLMNH.)

Use of net mesh gauge being demonstrated by Mitchell Hope. (Photo by William Marquardt.)

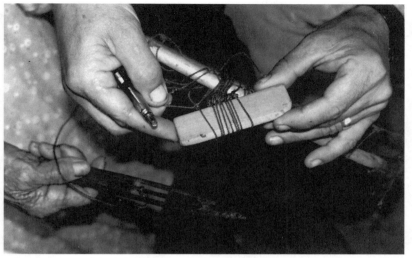

Esperanza Woodring gives me a lesson, using a precolumbian net mesh gauge. (Photo by Karen Walker.)

motor was mounted in a tunnel towards the front of the boat so as not to interfere with the net. They could travel in only inches of water, giving them access to the shallow bays. They were also faster and could cover much more territory.

Cast *nets*, according to Goode (pp. 34-35), were primitive devices introduced to the area by Spaniards but used much more extensively in Sarasota Bay than in Charlotte Harbor.

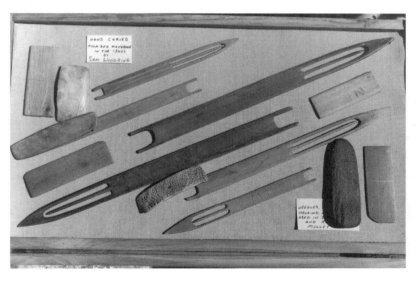

Net mesh gauges and shuttles made by Esperanza Woodring's husband set beside precolumbian artifacts for comparison. (Photo by Karen Walker.)

Trammel nets, first used in this area in the 1940s, are like gill nets but have two to three layers of netting. The inner layer has smaller mesh. It also uses float and weight lines like the seine net. It is used to gill different sizes of fish in one net. They were adapted locally to "wingding" off the Gulf beaches for pompano, a technique where the net is stretched offshore and the end is curled into a spiral where fish are gilled when they "strike" the net trying to escape. They are also used to strike a moving school of fish, such as trout or redfish, in open water.

A *trawl net* is weighted with a purse for holding the catch that is dragged behind a boat over the bottom. In this area, trawl nets are used mainly for catching shrimp and scallops.

Net Floats

Net floats were made from wood, gourds, hollow glass balls, cork, and now plastics. Floats were tied at the top across the full length of stop nets, seine nets, and trammel nets.

Tom Parkinson

Well, you know, when my father first came down here [1890s] and started fishing, all the floats were wood. They were made out of something like gumbo limbo; they are real light. All that he had were tarred, and I know in later years when they started getting Spanish corks, he did not use them anymore. Us kids used them to play baseball with them. It would take about a dozen because you'd bust one about every three or four times you would hit it. But there were some of

them [that were] long and some of them were round.

Net Mesh Gauges

Net mesh gauges, locally called "paddles," are used in net making and mending to determine the net mesh stretch size. Before the introduction of plastic net mesh gauges, Charlotte Harbor's senior fisherfolk used gauges made from red mangrove and other native woods. Archaeological gauges made of shell, bone, and wood have been recognized (Marquardt 1992b; Walker 1992) in southwest Florida. Their width measurements can be translated easily into actual net-mesh stretch sizes. The precolumbian net mesh gauges found in the Charlotte Harbor area are of sizes that could have been used for making stop nets, seine nets, dip nets, and gill nets. The larger of these gauges approximate the sizes required by the twentieth-century mullet fishery for gill nets. Most of the larger fish as well as smaller fish (such as pinfish, spot, and pigfish) represented in the mounds could have been caught easily with nets made using such gauges. Many large fish (trout, redfish, mullet) could also have been taken from these small-mesh nets with dip nets, spears, or other means.

During the interviews, Charlotte Harbor fisherfolk discussed the early twentieth-century evolution of fishing nets.

Nellie Coleman

Everything came on the run boat. They ordered the nets for the fishermen, and we hung it in [tied the lead line and the float line to the netting] when it got down here. I was pretty small at the time. I didn't do much of it. I can still remember the first time they tried to teach me to mend them—I didn't like it. But after I got married that was a different story. I did most of the mending. There were cotton nets and flax nets. By the time the monofilament nets came in, the cotton and flax nets almost went out. I always dyed my nets pink or red, because there was so much red stuff in the water.

We had [nets]... one for every size [fish] and every season, although I did mostly trout fishing with a trammel net. But I did fish for mullet, too. They're all expensive, especially the trammel net, 'cause you got three walls you got to buy and hang in there. I hate hanging nets and mending nets, and, when I got out of it, I swore I'd never do it again. If you have a net, you have to keep working on it. It's like a boat and a motor. There's always something wrong with it; you have to keep working on it. No matter what kind you got.

Raymond Lowe, Sr.

The only thing we had was flax net and cotton net. In the fall of the year we fished four-inch 920 cotton or four-inch 18 flax. It was fine, and flax was soft, you know, but if we would have had glass nets, the way they tell me it catches fish, there wouldn't have been any fish left. We would've caught them all!

Tom Parkinson

[Stop nets were] set on high tides [and were] used to block off an area. We gathered fish from pot holes as the tide dropped using other nets [seines and cast nets] to remove the fish. We pulled up on a bank net [a seine net with no floats or weights] to remove fish from the pocket. [They were] made of cotton and tarred.

Grady Sands

There wasn't much stretch to them cotton [gill] nets. At first it would, but after it was wet and shrunk up, there wasn't much stretch to it. If you tried to push a mullet through it, you'd pop it [the mesh] every time.

Bo Smith

[Trammel nets] were used for pompano fishing with 4¼-inch mesh and #9 trammeling, used for "wing-dinging" and striking fish. Some had 208 twine and #9 walls for larger or stronger fish [redfish, trout, snook, etc.]

[I] started fishing for mullet in summer [with a gill net]. A 3⅝-inch [in the summer], then a 3⅞-inch and a 4-inch stretch mesh for roe season.

[Seine nets were] pulled on the beach. [They had a] 1 to 1½-inch stretch mesh. Made with #6 cotton twine for the wing and #9 for the bunt [pocket]. They were limed and spread after use to prevent rotting. [Stop nets] were tarred so the crabs couldn't eat them up.

Esperanza Woodring

See, these fish [mullet] used to come in, in schools, and they would take these huge big [seine] nets and rope them in....a great big heavy, long, and real deep seine. [They were] cotton. Oh, there was no such thing as flax in those days. [I used a monofilament] cast net, but not a gill net. When I quit [commercial] fishing, the last net I had was made out of flax.

Well, I think they used to have a beach or something to back them up, because they had to haul those fish up [with a seine]. See, those mullet did not gill in the net at all. It was a small-mesh net, so they just roped them in like a blanket or something.

Most of them [stop nets] were cotton [or flax], and they took and put them in tar to preserve them. The crabs ate them anyway, but not quite as bad.

If you were a fisherman, you had to know how to do a little bit of everything. I used to make cast nets, but not gill nets. There is too much work for those. We did all of our own work [hung them in]. We ordered most of ours from New York from a company. The name of them was W. A. Auger in New York. I still have some of their advertisements.

At one time we had some sheds down there that we used to keep our nets in that we did not use. We would have about three different sizes [for mullet]. One about an inch-and-a-quarter [stretch mesh]. Then when we were going to use it for the roe season, as they called it when they were spawning, it would be a larger net. That would be about...Oh, I do not remember exactly, but it would be a much larger mesh. The little fish would go through, and we would just catch the mother mullet, which was an awful thing to do.

We make our paddles out of wood. The needles, too. These are antique [net-mesh gauges and shuttles, or netting needles]. All that stuff Ralph's dad [Sam Woodring] made. He made that [net-mesh gauge] out of red mangrove root. I do not know why he used the red mangrove. I guess he used it because he thought it preserved or kept better. Let me show you the [mending] needles that we used to make. You can buy them for much cheaper than you can make them anymore [see photograph, page 137].

[Esperanza's early twentieth-century net-mesh gauges are the same sizes as some of the precolumbian net mesh gauges we brought to show her: 3", 3½", 4"].

[Do] you know how they pulled the nets out of the boat? They had this great big thing, I think you would call it a wheel, I suppose. It was made out of palmetto stalks or wood or whatever they could find. It was up on the forks like this, see, and then this thing would roll on these forks. That is the way they would pull the net in to repair it or put it out or anything. I do not think they had lime in those days. If they did, I do not remember. Well, I guess my dad had lime for his nets, but I am pretty sure they started [liming their nets].

They used stop nets to go along the edge, like on that island over there. They are not that deep, because they did not use those in deep water. They used the island like a background. See that island over there? Well, when the tide is low, all of that goes dry in there underneath those mangroves. See, there are little dips in the ground, and there would be little puddles of water. They would get [trapped] in there [and they would get them] with a dip net or a cast net.

Elmer Johnson

We done stop netting in the bays, gill netting, and used seines too. We used about two or three. We put out a thousand of yards of net. We used to catch them by the thousands, you know. We used to "stop" big nets. I caught a hundred and ten thousand [pounds] in one stop. Seine nets, that's what I pulled. We had to dry the cotton ones...Gill nets have been used here hundreds of years. The trammel net came from the Carolinas. They had them there, and somebody moved down here with them, and we started using them.

Alfonso Darna

That stop net is sometimes a half-mile long. It is pulled on a bank net made of heavy twine that is tarred.

Shucked oyster meats are shown
in a quahog clam shell placed
upon a bed of oyster shells.
(Photo by Robin Brown.)

CHAPTER 9

Shellfish

Oysters

Oysters (*Crassostrea virginica*) build reefs in the bays and mangrove-fringed tidal creeks of Charlotte Harbor. Oysters are tolerant of significant changes in water temperature, salinity, tide, turbidity, and pollution (Seaman 1985:251, 254). They are well adapted to Charlotte Harbor's estuarine conditions and are the most common species of shellfish found there. Oysters were gathered for personal consumption by all of my informants.

Surplus oysters were generally traded, bartered, or given away. Commercial harvesting of oysters, as well as oyster seeding of maintained bars, was attempted during the Depression of the 1930s, but without much success. Larger, more robust oysters, harvested commercially, require more temperate waters. They are harvested mainly to the north of Charlotte Harbor (Seaman 1985:285).

Oysters represented a food resource for the harbor's original inhabitants and also an important source of building material. Oyster shells appear to be the major component of many Indian mounds around Charlotte Harbor. Unusually large, robust oyster shells can be observed in vast quantities in the Calusa Island midden and a number of other Archaic-period sites in the harbor. These extra-large Archaic oyster shells suggest a somewhat cooler climate.

Small "coon oysters" (representing mangrove areas of collection), "bar oysters," and deep-water oysters were all collected and are represented at different sites at different times. Some have speculated that Native Americans may have practiced oyster aquaculture in the harbor. Oyster Shoals (west of Calusa Island), Turtle Bay, and Bull Bay oyster areas of Charlotte Harbor are very interesting prospects. The material sources for the archaeological sites around there were rich in oyster shell, as they still are today.

Tom Parkinson

Your oysters should still be pretty good [in April]. Large oyster beds were maintained by fishermen in Bull and Turtle Bays and commercially harvested [1930s]. [Now they're] on the decline from overfishing.

Bill Hunter

I eat oysters in January, February, and March; then I don't eat them—that is the end of them. By the middle of March they are full of roe, so I don't bother with them then. Many large ones are found in Turtle and Bull Bay.

Alfonso Darna

It seems like the oysters have more mud on them than there used to be. Maybe that is pollution. I do not know. It used to be that on these oyster bars the oysters would not be so muddy. Now you go to an oyster bar, and there is so much mud on them.

A lot of people got bad sick from eating them oysters after the 1947 red tide.

Raymond Lowe, Sr.

They sold them by the bushel. They had that place over there where that boat lift is; by the marina there [in Placida], but it didn't amount to nothing. They got quite a few oysters, but it sort of petered out. See oysters, they go and come; they're seasonal. One year you'll have a lot of oysters, and the next year something will kill them out and you don't have any. My brother-in-law, he worked over there, and I told him it won't work. He was a New Englander, where they grew them things, and it didn't amount to nothing. He said it would [work], but it didn't. It didn't last. They had that place over there seeded out, but I don't think that's the proper place to grow oysters. You have enough for the people; you see that's what I'm telling you about nature: there was enough oysters for everybody, they got to monkeying with it, and now you can hardly get a mess of oysters. It goes right back to people; there is just too many people. Places over the whole country is just overpopulated.

The best oysters, the best fish in the country, come out of this bay. Now they are polluting it. That's the trouble with the world right now. It's polluted, it's overpopulated, and they don't seem to do anything about it. There's not as many [oysters] now because too much pressure is on them. They don't get big any more.

Nellie Coleman

We ate quite a few of them. We didn't sell them when we got them. After the War [World War II], they cleaned them out. They didn't last long after they started getting them to sell. They had a factory at Matlacha where they hauled them to sell. They had regular shellers to shell the scallops, the oysters, and clams. But they got so scarce, they had to quit. Then they passed so many of the laws, you couldn't take them. They began to find diseases in them, or so they say. But I think it was 'cause people were eating them the wrong time of the year. They do it now too—they eat them the wrong time of the year—and they get sick and they blame them. They eat them raw. That's the worst thing you can do is eat shellfish raw!

Whether they're bad or not, they're bad for you anyway [raw]. You can get hepatitis from them. What other kind of diseases, I don't know. They're filtering stuff out of the water, and, if there is anything in the water, they are bound to get it. My parents were pretty old-fashioned. When the sun got hot, we didn't eat stuff like that.

Esperanza Woodring

Oysters are not very good [during the summer]. [Oysters are good] only in the winter time when it is cold.

Bo Smith

[I] never did any oyster-ing commercially. Well, I did in the wintertime sometimes if I needed [some extra money]. I got four or five dollars a bushel. I would just sell enough to pay for my expenses, and I would keep the rest. I never got more than a couple or three bushels full. I would just take what I wanted and maybe sell a bushel, like I said, to pay for my gas. Shoot, I could sit on the oyster bar and eat them raw right out of the water.

You do not get oysters till you get two or three cold spells on them. A lot of people go to get them, but they are just wasting them, you know. If you wait till the water gets pretty cold, then they get fat. The first of the year there are plenty of them. But so many people get them, you know, they clean them out.

I think that there are places with muddy bottoms you get them on, and then there are sandy bottoms, you know. The deep-water ones you get with tongs, they are mostly long oysters—long and narrow.

Grady Sands

You go down there and try to find you a mess of oysters now. They are not there. There are no oys-ters!

Clams

The southern quahog (*Mercenaria campechiensis*) is a bivalve found mainly in shallow sand/mud areas. It is usually partially buried in sand or mud with its shell slightly open for feeding. With a large muscular "foot" for burrowing, its flat body lies be-tween two muscles used for closing the shells and is covered by the man-tle. It has intake and outlet openings and feeds by siphoning nutrients from the water. Clams are edible and have been harvested in large quanti-ties by Charlotte Harbor's inhabi-tants through time.

During the winter months, when northeast winds cause extreme low tides, clams can be easily gathered. They can be seen spitting streams of water as the incoming tide returns. As water covers them again, there is a keyhole-like opening in the sand from their siphon that gives away their location. On higher tides "treading" the area with bare feet easily locates them in the sandy bottom. The pointed end of a medium-sized lightning-whelk shell poked into the bottom is also a convenient way of locating them. A shell-to-shell sound gives away their location. The whelk shell also can be used to dig them out.

Large whelks are common predators of clams and frequently can be found feeding on a captured victim. After locating and digging out the clam, the whelk opens the clam with its foot and the edge of its own shell. It then inserts its mouth, and digestive fluids are secreted in the shell, forming a mucus-like membrane that surrounds the animal. The clam is digested slowly over the next couple of days—clam on the half shell, whelk style.

While camping at Charlotte Harbor, my children tied a short line and a float to several large, live whelks by punching a small hole in the outer lip of the shells. The whelks were then returned to the bay bottom where they sought out live clams. Clams could easily be gathered by retrieving the whelk and removing the clam from its grasp. Care had to be taken to harvest the clam before the whelk put its foot in the door, so to speak. Once digestion began, the clam took on an entirely different taste and texture. (Who knows, it may once have been a cultural delicacy!)

Clams, an important resource to the Native American fisherfolk of Charlotte Harbor, were used for seasonal food in late winter and early spring (Quitmyer and Jones 1992:254-258). Indians fashioned many different kinds of tools from the large robust shells, such as anvils, pounders, choppers, digging tools, and net weights (Marquardt 1992b). They also had a special enigmatic significance as suggested by the fact that the right valve is almost always broken when found on a site; or the left valves are usually the only valve found intact (Luer 1986:132). This phenomenon marks a cultural preference of Native Americans in southwest Florida lasting from 5,000 years ago until well after the demise of the Calusa culture. This left-handed clam shell signature in the many shell deposits of Charlotte Harbor is a quick indicator of a site that was used by precolumbian people.

Tom Parkinson

Your clams would be good and fat. [April] is a good time for clams.

Bill Hunter

I eat clams all of the time, except for three months: January, February, and March [when] I eat oysters. You see, clams are spawning now [February].

We did not have any kind of commercial shellfish here [Boca Grande]. I got them to eat myself. I just got what I wanted. Everybody did that. If you wanted clams, you dug a dozen clams, and that was it. But today people will go out there and get two or three bushels of clams and only eat one.

Right in back of my house [on Captiva] I could get all the clams I wanted. You just step down there. I went barefooted. There are still plenty of clams [there].

Richard Coleman

Well, we never did get many shellfish in the fall of the year. Maybe in the wintertime we would get some oysters now and then, and maybe clams.

[Things like red tide are hard on] any kind of shellfish—clams, scallops, or oysters. Red tide works on them.

Esperanza Woodring

And the clams, we eat them most anytime of the year. We used to. I am afraid to eat a clam now unless I know exactly where they came from. There are so many bugs. The tourists are about to wreck the clam beds.

Bo Smith

Clams are good all year round. Now, in summertime clams are fatter. But clams [compared to oysters]—there are just millions of clams everywhere. [The Campbell Soup Company] would dredge them up and put them in croaker sacks. When I was fishing, I would go by and see croaker sacks all along there to the "Kitchen Flats," on the east side of Gasparilla Island where they had put them. They took the whole thing. At the end of the day, they would come by and pick up the croaker sacks full of clams. They had a little jet thing, and [it would] just jet them up. I never watched them do it. I mean, I have seen them do it, but I never went up to them. I think the government stopped it. Somebody stopped it. You could not get but so many, you know.

I have not really noticed them [clams] back in there [Bull and Turtle Bay], because I usually get them around these flats [around here]. You know, down there by the "Kitchen" [Gasparilla Sound, about midpoint on Gasparilla Island], there are bunches of them. Just outside the bayou there are bunches of them. That bar, there are plenty of clams on it. On Three Sisters [Island] over there—there are plenty [of clams].

Grady Sands

Now, [as for] clams, that section of the bottom right there in front of the fish house [the Gasparilla Fishery in Placida], as I understand, is supposed to be closed [to shellfish collectors] because the pollution coming from the marina on the ebb tide goes across it. And I will bet you that damn shrimp boat up there, that big one [the *Gasparilla VI*], could make four trips and never haul the damn clams that have been took off that [bar] out there. Nobody has ever been sick. You can go right across the channel and get all you want [legally] if they are there. It is not closed [to shellfishers]. What the hell is the difference? I do not know. I cannot figure it out.

Scallops

Scallops (Pectinidae) periodically come into the estuaries through the Gulf passes to the grass flats in the warmer months (May - October). They are still commercially harvested in Pine Island Sound by shallow-draft trawlers dragging the grass flats at night. The scallop fishery was damaged by the construction of the Sanibel causeway in 1963 and by dredging of canals and waterways in the 1950s and 1960s (Haddad and Hoffman 1986:184; Harris et al. 1983:134).

Concentrations of scallop shells found on archaeological sites may be a seasonal indicator, since scallops are mostly available at certain times of the year.

Tom Parkinson

They [scallops] were common not too many years ago but were overfished.

Bill Hunter

I drug scallops over in Pine Island Sound—that was the best place.

I used to make money from scallops. Back in the 1930s we used to get a dollar a bushel. There were scallops all up and down this coast here. I got scallops over in Pine Island Sound [by Captiva Pass]. That was the best place. There were more scallops there than anywhere else. It was before the cool weather, like August, September, October. I did have some scallop nets, but I do not have them now. You could make twelve or fifteen dollars a day. I'll tell you there were scallops all up and down [the inside] of Cayo Costa, up and down the coast [in the Gulf] too.

During the war [World War II] they seemed to disappear.

Alfonso Darna

There are still a few scallops in the bay just across from Redfish and Captiva Pass.

Richard Coleman

There were a lot of scallops around here, whenever you wanted to eat some, you just dipped them up with a dip net.

Raymond Lowe, Sr.

We collected them [scallops] to eat. They were everywhere, all you wanted. Now you can't find one.

Nellie Coleman

We didn't sell them, but we ate lots of scallops. They were dipped with a net. There were lots of them until they started dredging for them commercially in the 1950s and when they built the Sanibel Causeway [in 1962], that changed the water flow.

Esperanza Woodring

We used to get some to eat up on Tarpon Bay [Sanibel Island] at low water. You used to could go up there and pick them up by the washtub full. [But] not commercially. We picked them up with our hands. One bit him [Ralph] one time. He got so mad he squashed that scallop. He was just a tot you know. Oh, he was so mad. It made his finger bleed. Boy, he was a mad kid.

Up until the time they built that causeway [there were scallops]. That fixed all the scallops in this section of the world. In 1962, I think, they opened the damned thing [the Sanibel causeway].

Bo Smith

Here on Big Flats [by Hogan's Key, near mid-Gasparilla Island] when I was a kid, we used to take a skiff and pull it along. Two or three people would pick them up as fast as they could. There used to be the most scallops you ever saw come in there. One time we went across to Pine Island. The scallops must have been moving, 'cause out in the middle of the Pass [Captiva Pass], it was just solid with them. We took a little dip net and dipped the stern of the boat full of them. They don't get back in there in Pine Island Sound since they built that Sanibel Causeway.

Penshells

Two species of penshells (Pinnidae) are found in the area: the stiff penshell (*Atrina rigida*) found in the bays and Gulf and the saw-toothed penshell (*Atrina serrata*) found in the Gulf (Abbott 1974:438-439).

As a food source, penshells contain a large scallop-like muscle. It is a very tender delicacy, especially when eaten raw, but penshells quickly acquire a taste of iodine if not eaten or processed quickly. Cooking toughens the meat somewhat, but penshells still retain their sweet taste. Pounding the meat also tenderizes it, but it is not necessary. They are eaten by many local people but have never had a commercial value.

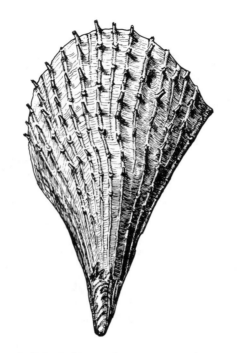

Pen shell. Scale: ½ actual size. (Drawing by Merald Clark.)

They are known locally as "pearl oysters," because of the iridescent luster of the shell. After storms, thousands of pen shells are uprooted and wash up on local beaches, many still alive. Such events might represent opportunities to gather them in the large numbers we see represented in the archaeological sites.

Penshells are found in many Native American mounds in the Charlotte Harbor area, including Buck Key, Josslyn Island, Big Mound Key, and Useppa, to name a few. They have been found in thick isolated stratified layers (e.g., Buck Key), and mixed in with other shell throughout other mound matrix. They often appear to have been gathered, when available, in large quantities.

The thread-like hair, called "byssus," which anchors the pen shell in the bottom mud, is sometimes locally referred to as "sea silk." It is possible that byssus was used by the precolumbian inhabitants for cordage because of the fineness of the thread, its strength, and iridescent colors. This species is known and used world-wide for its specialized fiber.

This material has not been found in archaeological sites to date. We should look for it in waterlogged contexts such as those of the Pineland site. It is very unlikely that the byssus was discarded by the aboriginal fisherfolk, because it represented an important fiber source.

The following excerpt is from Captain Mike Fuery's *Florida Shelling Guide* (1982:35):

The tuft is called a "byssal" and back in Roman times it was collected from live pens (which are found over most parts of the world in warmer waters) and spun into thread. Back many years ago, this thread was referred to as being "sea silk" and was expensive to produce. It made extremely fine fabric when the threads were woven, and it was given for use to only the most wealthy and famous. The process died out sometime around the first part of the century.

There is an old saying among local people that you can tell how bad a storm was by how many live penshells washed ashore. I've walked the beaches after storms where there were thousands of dying and dead penshells on the beach (field notes; Storm-of-the-Century, March 12-13, 1993). I collected many penshells for the byssus tufts and food at this time.

Tom Parkinson

We call them "pearl oysters." They wash up after storms on the beach. Many are still alive. The hairs are called "sea silk."

Bill Hunter

Pearl oysters, I've eat them, but, like you said, they're tough.

Alfonso Darna

I have tried them, oh, maybe two or three of them. I think they are tough. The other scallops do not get that way.

Richard Coleman

Oh, yes [I've eaten them]. I have got them once or twice out there in that middle ground, that hole in the wall flat [the east side of mid-Gasparilla Island]. There used to be one hell of a lot of them. They are kind of like a scallop.

Esperanza Woodring

Yes [I've eaten penshells]. They are delicious. There are not many around anymore. Even they have deteriorated. There used to be a lot of them around. When we lived on Cayo Costa, there was an old woman over there. They used to call her a witch. She used to take that hair and clean it, and then if she had an ear ache or any kind of ache, she would put some kind of junk in that hair and put it on there. I do not know whether it did any good or not, but if you believe in it, I guess it helps. But she swore that was good. It is pretty strong, you know. You cannot hardly break it. We used to take it when we were kids and make mustaches out of it.

Tarpon fishing boats in Boca Grande Pass during tarpon tournament, 1992. (Photo courtesy of Boca Beacon.)

CHAPTER 10

Lifetime Changes

The destruction of marine habitat, changes in the environment due to pollution, increases in population, and new legislation and regulations—all these factors have affected the lives of Charlotte Harbor's senior fisherfolk. Their world view is based on their life experiences and gives us a look at when these changes occurred and their responses to them. I asked my informants, "What are the biggest changes in commercial fishing you have seen in your lifetime?" and "What changes have you seen in the harbor?" Their answers all date to 1994 or earlier, before the 1995 net ban took effect.

Tom Parkinson

The independent commercial fisherman is a dying breed. Too many laws are made by people who don't know the area or the local people. Every new law hurts the local commercial fishermen and favors the sports fishermen.

I hate to see it happen on account of fishermen has always been my kind of people, but I think you'll see where they'll finally put an end to it.

Things are happening so quickly now you don't stop to think about it. Back when I first started fishing I had a little old slow twenty-foot launch to tow a couple or three skiffs out. I'd camp over in Bulls Bay and go up to Cape Haze Point and Turtle Bay and it would take all day. Now they get in there with these fast kickerboats and they can fish all the way up to Punta Gorda and back just as quick.

Old Everett Tucker and Edgar Gaines was the first to fish those [outboard] "kickerboats" down here [in Boca Grande] and the biggest complain was from down there [at the fishery in Placida]. They used little old "launches" with inboard motors in them [to tow out the pole skiffs]. They tried their best to get "warmed up" [mad] about them [outboard motors]. The said, "them kickerboats, even if they run by you way out and give lots of leeway, the exhaust in the water will run the fish off." Now they [the fishermen] all got them!

A lot of things just don't seem right. I know growth means prosperity and I'm not against growth, but they're just going to have to control it somehow.

Even the most ignorant person would realize that sports fishing is worth more to the economy than commercial fishing. So why don't the state just come right out and say it!

Now down there at the [fish house] dock one day "they" [the sports fishermen] were talking about being sports fishermen and what the commercial fishermen had done [to the fishing]. I said, "do you consider yourselves sports fishermen?" He said, "Oh yeah, I've got a boat and I go out fishing every weekend." And I said, "A sports fisherman in my eyes is one who comes down here and stays at the "hotel" [Gasparilla Inn], hires one of these guide boats and goes out there fishing and if he has a good day he'll tip the captain fifty or seventy-five dollars." I said, "Now that's what I call a sports fisherman!"

You know, years back, and it hasn't been too many years back, the ordinary working man could not afford a boat, motor and trailer and a trip every weekend. Now they all got them!

For every fish you take out of the sea there's one less fish in the sea. It don't matter if he jumps in the boat, he's not out there anymore.

It comes down to one thing, it's people, there just too many people now.

I had a friend over in Punta Gorda who fished mostly for pompano. If you asked his kids if he was a fisherman they would say no, he's a "pompano fisherman." That was a little higher class.

You know, fishermen has always been thought of as an uneducated bunch of people, because way back their parents didn't have much education. It was pretty tough for everybody in those days. Now you take over there in Placida, there are still families over there that never did anything but fish. Their children all have at least a high school education. There ain't a one of those places you don't see an automobile and a television. Now you take old Fonso [Darna], I'll bet he never made a nickel in his life he didn't make from fishing!

As a boy born and raised here, it took me half to two-thirds of my working life to ac-

cumulate enough to build a home and that's after buying property back long enough to where you could pay it off little at a time.

Someone told me that old "Tee Wee" [Arnold Joiner] was going to have to quit fishing. He just couldn't make enough money to carry a lawyer along with him [on the boat] to tell him when, where, and how to fish.

Sawfish were very common when I was a boy in Charlotte Harbor. I remember large schools of them in the bay, and they used to tear up our nets. You don't see them any more.

There were hundreds of thousands of blue crabs where there are none now.

I have not seen a sawfish in thirty years. There used to be lots of them. If you walked along the beach, you used to see hundreds of the little ones.

People didn't catch up all the fish, it's the outboards, red tide, and things like that. Of course if they quit catching them with their nets during roe season at least they'd get to spawn.

Fishing ain't no good anymore. They got to do more than collect data on it, they've got to get out there and get with it.

Bill Hunter

I will tell you where the biggest problem is in losing fish and all of the resources that we have, and there is nothing that anyone can do about it. It is the outboard kicker boats. They put more pollution in the water than any other thing in the whole world. As long as you have a motor that operates on an oil and gasoline mixture [outboard], some of it is going to go into the water. The devil can tell you [it is] true.

Alfonso Darna

I do not see much change in them areas [Bull and Turtle Bays], except for the lack of fish.

I have noticed this moss, what we call "rolling moss." It is just old, yellow mossy grass. I notice more of that in Turtle Bay and Bull Bay than at any time [in the past]. There is more now than I have ever seen. You can hardly strike for it. Sometimes it is that deep [knee high]. When you strike now, your lead line is laying right in that grass, and the fish go right under that lead line. You cannot even hit bottom for it. You can hardly get it [the net] in your boat it is so thick [with rolling moss].

There were more, lots more, blue crabs [back then]. Now, they got scarce, too. I do not know what happened to them. Usually, man, you could hardly fish for them. Louis [Darna] and I came in here at Cape Haze Bayou. Let me see, it was Louis and I and Raymond Rodriguez and Eugene Hamilton. We struck in there, and we just met the compass [made a full circle], you know. I went back to the let-go [the end of the net with the weight on it] to clear it. It looked like it was sunk. I just picked it up, and it was just plum full of blue crabs. We had to rope it in [pull it to the boat] right quick. I mean, we did not even leave the nets overboard twenty minutes, and we had over three-hundred head of blue crabs in that net. We did not strike in there anymore. You could not hardly fish in there. See, the only fishing that was going on mostly in those islands then—Turtle Bay and Bull Bay— was [done by] stop-netters [for mullet]. They used heavy tarred, big solid nets, and the crabs would not eat them.

There were more sawfish here years ago. On the beach you would catch the real big ones [while pompano fishing] and in the bays you would catch them [small ones] in the gill nets. I have not seen another one since the one we caught [when we fished together in 1982].

Richard Coleman

The nets are the biggest change, I guess. They used to use cotton nets when I started, and now they use these glass [monofilament] nets. We used to have to mend nets all the time, but now they do not mend them [much] anymore.

It is funny how we used to go out here in these skiffs. We did not have any ice at all in the boat. We would go out before sundown—the sun would still be up—and we would not come in the next morning until the sun was up. Those fish were in that skiff all night long, with hot water in there, and we had no trouble at all selling those fish— all of them. Now you would never think of buying fish like that. You would say they were rotten. Well, of course, if we sold them

right here [Boca Grande], they would bring them in and ice them down. They already would be roughed up [bruised]. Then they would ship them to Georgia or Alabama and sell them all right. Now you have to carry ice with you and throw them right on the ice.

Raymond Lowe, Sr.

We talk about that a lot. I don't think there is as many mullet as there used to be, but on the same token we got so much traffic on the bay all the time, and the fish can't gather up like they used to.

The fishing has really changed, the type of nets, the type of boats. I think you got a different type of people than what you used to have [here].

If we would have had glass [monofilament] nets when we was fishing, there wouldn't be any fish left. We would have caught them all! The only thing we had was flax net and cotton net. There was plenty of blue crabs in those days. [You] almost can't hardly catch one now.

Things have changed over the years. Everybody has their own ideas—modern man and ancient man too. Man has gotten to messing with nature and, when you do this, you get in trouble. That's what's wrong with us now. We mess with nature, and it won't work. As long as you let nature take care of itself, well, nature's one of the greatest, finest things ever. If you would study it, just stop, think, look and listen, it's one of the greatest things there is. But man, he's got to mess with it, correct it. "Nature ain't doing just right," so we got to correct it a little bit... [but] then we're in trouble!

Not too long ago, this was the biggest unpolluted bay in the country—Charlotte Harbor Bay. Now they are starting to pollute it. You got all these chemicals leaching into the bay; and it's the same way with Lake Okeechobee. All that stuff is leaching off those farms back in there, and after it reaches Okeechobee it's just killing it. They're going to do something about it, but when? When it's dead!

The worst thing that ever happened to Boca Grande was that bridge coming over here. But you're glad they got it when you have to go to town in a hurry. It used to be, going to town was an all-day affair. You'd catch the ferry and get to the other side

about nine o'clock. Then you'd go do your shopping early and whatever. Then you would have to wait 'til that evening to come back. It was an all-day affair.

There is so many people, so much traffic all the time. The boys tell me, "You have to pick a chance to get across the inland waterway out there." It's like crossing the street. We didn't used to have that. They ought to outlaw them damn kicker boats [outboard motor boats].

Nellie Coleman

 All this spraying [against mosquitos] and stuff hurt a lot of the land turtles, the fish, and water. I remember when they [Lee County Mosquito Control] first started spraying these canals here. There used to be a lot of minnows and fish right here in these canals [in Bokeelia]. I remember the first time they came down here and started spraying; it killed them, and they ain't been many back much since.

[When the scallops disappeared] they didn't know what caused it, whether it was the [Sanibel] causeway or something in the

water. I think [it was] the causeway, because it changed the tides, and then they didn't come in anymore. The last few years there's been a few come in, but not like they used to. I don't remember what year it was [the scallops disappeared], but it was sometime after World War II. It was around the time they put in that Sanibel causeway [1963].

There's too many fishermen, and there's a decline in fish. But it's not from the fishing. The fish are just not right. It's not because you're catching them [all], it's just because they're not multiplying. Their natural habitats like Cape Coral—that was a natural habitat in there—but they went in and built all those canals, and there's no place for them to raise their young. The mangroves are all gone. It's the same way as here [Bokeelia]. Like up on Burnt Store Road, they went and dug all those canals; that was a natural habitat, and they destroyed all that.

They did a lot of damage, too, dragging for bait shrimp. See, for their bait, they used to catch them [shrimp] with lights and dip nets. When they started that dragging, you could tell the difference, 'cause they dragged all over the bay, and the fish didn't come back there. There wasn't nothing there for them to eat.

I think the glass nets is what ruined the fishing. I don't know if they could see it or not, but they caught bigger fish [with them], and the bigger fish is what had the roe. By time it come roe season, why, they didn't leave enough for seed.

Esperanza Woodring

Earl [Johnson] used to be a fisherman and a guide. Now he cannot even catch a fish to eat [laughter]. [Now] it is unbelievable. There was no time that I could not go out there at the head of the dock and get a mess of fish, clean them, and cook them for dinner that night. I have been out there [fishing] for three or four days [now] and did not even lose a shrimp. That is unbelievable! I never thought I would see the day that I could not go out on the head of my dock and get a mess of fish.

There's too many fishermen. That is part of the game. Then the red tide kills a lot [of fish]. And the powerboats go over these flats where the fish lay their little eggs; they churn the mud up and kill the grass roots and stuff like that. That is the reason why all

Esperanza Woodring's dock. (Photo by Karen Walker.)

the stuff is deteriorating, because they [the fish] do not have enough place to protect themselves. The channels have changed, and they are deeper than they were. There is no place for a fish to live or feed. There is nothing there for them to stay for. There is nothing out there but white sand. They either die or leave. I guess down around the Everglades and that section, probably, the

fishing down there is not quite so bad as it is here. But they will take care of it eventually [people will destroy it].

I think that if a fish is left alone and the feed is there, I think they stay there unless something comes and disturbs them or the feed disappears. Like you, you are not going to stay where you cannot eat. That is the way it is with the fish. If you feed them and do not scare them, they are all right. They'll stay there, at least I think. Only maybe when they go to spawn or have sex or something like that, I imagine they must have certain places that they go [then]. I do not know.

Bo Smith

Well, the only change, really, is the way they are fishing now. They got these kicker boats, you know, and they just go everywhere.

What has helped these fishermen now, I think, is glass [monofilament] nets.

It is just easier fishing [with a glass net]. With cotton nets, we had to wrap them up, close them up, and then drive them in the net. Sometimes we had to rope them down, you know. With glass nets, you just have to see which way they're going and strike them. Just run that thing out [and] around them. You do not even have to close it up. Just run it the way they are going.

You could catch anything back then. If you wanted to go trout fishing, you could catch trout. If you wanted to go grouper fishing, you could catch grouper. Just whatever you wanted to fish for, you could catch.

I know the scallops have not been back in [around] Pine Island since they built that bridge across to Sanibel. They used to come in there, you know, but you do not get many scallops over there anymore.

There are a lot less [blue crabs] now. [At one time] I could not strike with my net without them eating it up. Like in Turtle Bay and Bull Bay, if you ever put your net around a bunch of mullet, you had better get it up right now! Just rope it in.

Charlie Downing (center) receiving tarpon tournament trophy. Sport fishing has a long history in the Charlotte Harbor area, dating back to the late nineteenth century. Today there are more sport fishers than ever before. (Photo courtesy of Boca Beacon.)

Grady Sands

I think back in my early time there were more fish... but there's more fishermen now. You take back when the early fishermen like me and my dad and my uncle [were fishing]. We could go out there at night and if we struck and did not catch but thirty head of fish, what the hell. That was thirty head. We would get up and go again. We always put our fish together; they all went on one ticket [when we sold them to the fish house]. Then we split it [the proceeds] between us.

I think right now if they outlawed all those outboard motors, you would see a difference. There is no habitat nowhere on the bottom for the fish to feed on. It is all cut up [by the propellors of the outboards]. Another thing, for every six gallons of gas, [two-cycle outboards require] a pint of oil. Where does that oil go? Now they tried to tell me that oil floats. I am going to give you an example. There is not nothing we can do about it, because money has got it, [and] money is going to fight it. [You know] right over there where they test those damned motors [Mercury motors test center in Placida], I can carry you over there right now. Oh, hell, fifty foot behind where they are running, I can stick my oar down, and when it hits, you can just keep poking it [further down]. The oil is that [knee] deep on the damn bottom. But they say that there is nothing we can do about it. Think about it. Of course, it is not only the commercial fishermen that are cutting all of this grass and stuff off of the bottom. It is the sport fishermen as well as anything else. The boat traffic here is so pathetic that it is pitiful. And the only thing that caused that—of course, if that one hadn't, somebody else would—is that damn marina right there [Gasparilla Marina in Placida].

Elmer Johnson

[It was] many a year, a good long time before I got one [a power boat]. We all poled our boats or sailed them.

[Now there's] too many people! For every commercial fisherman you got five hundred recreational fishermen. That's what most people don't understand, we got one boat and they have hundreds of boats, tearing up the grass, wasting the gasoline and everything else. It's such a small place, you know?

We used to have sawfish here [Estero Bay] by the dozens and they were thick... I've caught small ones and big ones, we had them both. We used to have sharks in the bay here seven and eight foot long, you don't see them anymore.

Mamie Weeks

I've seen it changed so much! It's nothing like it used to be here [in Estero Bay]. It has really changed so much...and it took years to do it.

Commercial fishing boat at anchor off Cayo Costa, ca. 1910. A mullet net is piled at the stern of the boat. (Photo courtesy of Richard Coleman.)

Epilogue

The vitality of Charlotte Harbor's marine resources directly affects the future of the commercial and recreational fishing industries. The senior fisherfolk watched the environment and its marine resources deteriorate in their lifetimes. The present generation of commercial fisherfolk can no longer count on the bounty of the marine environment for their sustenance.

A state ban on entanglement nets went into effect in July, 1995, severely restricting their livelihoods. To survive, they will have to be more diverse in their endeavors. In the past century, sport fishing and related industries have supplemented the livelihood of commercial fisherfolk. The fisherfolk's traditional way of life, one that has existed in various forms in the Charlotte Harbor area for more than six thousand years, is

quickly passing. The fresh local seafood they provide, as well as the fish that the sport fishing industry relies on, are declining. As a result, the local economy is losing both an important food and a recreational resource.

These oral histories confirm that fishing has always played an integral role in the local economy. Now the harbor, its resources, and the people who make their livelihood from it need our protection.

Recent action taken by the Florida Legislature will determine the future of Charlotte Harbor's resources and those who make a living from them. As I write this epilogue, commercial fisherfolk are fighting a state constitutional amendment that threatens to annihilate the commercial fishing industry.

In my view, environmental stewards should see that local marine resources are equally distributed among groups who make their livelihoods from these resources. This must include both the sportfishing industry and the commercial fishery.

Today, as one group blames the other for its shortcomings, the real problems are loss of habitat and water pollution, a situation recognized by several of my informants. The recreational fishing industry, with its powerful lobbying groups, has targeted certain fish species and specific areas for its own use. For the commercial fishing industry to survive, it must have access both to certain species of food fish and to special areas. Local fisherfolk must demand habitat protection, clean water, and a share of the bounty of Charlotte Harbor.

Reflecting on what I learned from the senior fisherfolk, I believe they feel the following topics are relevant:

- The number of commercial licenses should be limited. New licenses should be available only by purchasing an existing license. The intrinsic value placed on these licenses would supplement an industry lacking disability and unemployment insurance or retirement plans.

- Some of the back bays, such as those around the Cape Haze Peninsula and Pine Island Sound, should be reserved as commercial fishing areas. Limiting the number of people fishing these areas and the types of boats and equipment used would help protect endangered habitats.

Mullet represents the most important species to the local fishery. Many of their habitats, such as canals and channels, are off-limits already to commercial fishing.

- Grouper has traditionally been an important commercial enterprise. The shallow-water "live bottom zone" located off the coast of southwest Florida could provide an exclusive area reserved for the commercial fishery (much as artificial reefs are reserved already for recreational fishing).

- Aquaculture, the farming of clams, fish, and other marine products, should be pursued. If profitable, these products would augment the commercial harvest. Other species could be raised for restocking depleted areas. Nothing to do with fishing or farming

comes without substantial risk. Traditionally, fishermen only took from the sea without putting anything back. This practice needs to be reconsidered. If pollution and habitat destruction continue, we may have no choice but to "farm" our food fish.

◆ ◆ ◆

The dilemma of pollution and habitat destruction has to be addressed on all levels of government. The responsibility of the people of Florida is to elect legislators who will ensure unpolluted habitats that will be available for future generations. Nurturing and protecting the natural and cultural resources of the Charlotte Harbor area is the responsibility of everyone. Ultimately, the protection of these resources will be through the value we attribute to them.

Bibliography

Abbott, R. Tucker
1974 *American Seashells.* Van Nostrand Reinhold, New York.

Austin, Daniel F.
1980 Historically Important Plants of Southeastern Florida. *The Florida Anthropologist* 33:17-31.

Brown, Robin C.
1994 *Florida's First People.* Pineapple Press, Sarasota, Florida.

Blunt, E. and G. W. Bullen
1833 *American Coast Pilot: Containing Directions for the Principal Harbours, Capes, and Headlands, on the Coasts of North and South America.* Twelfth edition. New York.

Bullen, Ripley P. and Adelaide K. Bullen
1956 *Excavations on Cape Haze Peninsula, Florida.* Contributions of the Florida State Museum, Social Sciences 1. Gainesville.

Clausen, Carl J., A. D. Cohen, Cesare Emiliani, J. A. Holman, and J. J. Stipp
1979 Little Salt Spring, Florida: A Unique Underwater Site. *Science* 203:609-614.

Comp, G.S. and W. Seaman, Jr.
1985 Estaurine Habitat and Fishery Resources of Florida. In *Florida Aquatic Habitat and Fishery Resources,* edited by W. Seaman, Jr., pp. 337-435. American Fisheries Society, Kissimmee, Florida.

Covington, James W.
1959 Trade Relations Between Southwestern Florida and Cuba, 1600-1840. *Florida Historical Quarterly* 38:114-128.

Davis, Richard A. Jr., Stephen C. Knowles, and Michael J. Bland

  1989   Role of Hurricanes in the Holocene Stratigraphy of Estuaries: Examples from the Gulf Coast of Florida. *Journal of Sedimentary Petrology* 59(6):1052-1061.

Department of Environmental Protection, State of Florida

  n.d.   *Fishing Lines: Angler's Guide to Florida Marine Resources.* Department of Environmental Protection, Tallahassee, Florida.

Dickinson, Jonathan

  1985   *Jonathan Dickinson's Journal, or God's Protecting Providence, Being the Narrative of a Journey from Port Royal in Jamaica to Philadelphia, August 23, 1696 to April 1st, 1697.* Florida Classics Library, Port Salerno, Florida.

Edic, Robert F.

  1982   A Preliminary Survey of Big Mound Key. Ms. on file, Florida Museum of Natural History, Gainesville, Florida.
  1990   The Coral Creek Site (8CH15). Ms. on file, Florida Museum of Natural History, Gainesville, Florida.
  1992   Pioneer Fisherfolks of Southwest Florida's Barrier Islands: An Interview with Esperanza Woodring of Cayo Costa. *The Florida Anthropologist* 45:221-225.

Estevez, E. D., J.E. Miller, and J. Morris

  1984   *Charlotte Harbor Estuarine Ecosystem Complex and the Peace River: A Review of Scientific Information.* Report to Southwest Florida Regional Planning Council. Mote Marine Laboratory, Sarasota.

Forbes, James Grant

  1821   *Sketches, Historical and Topographical, of the Floridas.* New York. (Facsimile edition, University of Florida Press, 1964.)

Fuery, Mike

  1982   *Captain Mike Fuery's New Florida Shelling Guide Featuring Sanibel, Captiva and Many Other Barrier Islands.* Print Shop of the Islands, Sanibel Island, Florida.

Gauld, George

  1765   *An Account of the Surveys of Florida, &c.* London, England.

Gibson, Charles Dana
1982   *Boca Grande: A Series of Historical Essays.* Great Outdoors Publishing Company, St. Petersburg, Florida.

Goggin, John M. and William T. Sturtevant
1964   The Calusa: A Stratified Non-Agricultural Society (with Notes on Sibling Marriage). In *Explorations in Cultural Anthropology: Essays in Honor of George Peter Murdock,* edited by Ward Goodenough, pp. 179-219. McGraw-Hill, New York.

Goode, G. George
1844-1887 *The Fisheries and Fishery Industries of the United States.* U. S. Government Printing Office, Washington, D.C.

Grant, Foreman
1953   *Indian Removal: The Emigration of the Five Civilized Tribes.* University of Oklahoma Press, Norman.

Haddad, Kenneth D. and Barbara A. Hoffman
1986   Charlotte Harbor Habitat Assessment. In *Managing Cumulative Effects in Florida Wetlands: Conference Proceedings.* Environmental Studies Program, New College of the University of South Florida, E.S.P. Publication 38. Sarasota.

Hann, John H.
1991   *Missions to the Calusa.* Introduction by William H. Marquardt, translations by John H. Hann. University Presses of Florida, Gainesville.

Harris, B. A., K. D. Haddad, K. A. Steidinger, J. A. Huff, and M. Y. Hedgepeth
1983   *Assessment of Fisheries Habitat: Charlotte Harbor and Lake Worth, Florida.* Florida Department of Natural Resources, St. Petersburg, Florida.

Harvey, Judson
1979   *Beach Processes and Inlet Dynamics in a Barrier-Island Chain, Southwest Florida.* Environmental Studies Program, New College of the University of South Florida, E.S.P. Publication 22. Sarasota.

Herwitz, Stanley

1977   *The Natural History of Cayo Costa Island.* Environmental Studies Program, New College of the University of South Florida, E.S.P. Publication 14. Sarasota.

Kerrigan, Anthony (editor)

1951   *Barcia's Chronological History of the Continent of Florida.* University of Florida Press, Gainesville.

Kozuch, Laura

1993   *Sharks and Shark Products In Prehistoric South Florida.* Monograph 2, Institute of Archaeology and Paleoenvironmental Studies, University of Florida, Gainesville.

Luer, George M.

1982   Archaeological Salvage of the Big Mound Key Site. Ms. on file, Florida Museum of Natural History, Gainesville, Florida.

1986   Some Interesting Archaeological Occurrences of Quahog Shells on the Gulf Coast of Central and Southern Florida. In *Shells and Archaeology in Southern Florida*, edited by George Luer, pp. 125-159. Florida Anthropological Society, Publication 12. Tallahassee.

Matthews, Janet S.

1983   *Edge of Wilderness: A Settlement History of Manatee River and Sarasota Bay, 1528-1885.* Caprine Press, Tulsa, Oklahoma.

Marquardt, William H.

1988   Politics and Production among the Calusa of South Florida. In *Hunters and Gatherers*, volume 1: *History, Evolution, and Social Change*, edited by Tim Ingold, David Riches, and James Woodburn, pp. 161-188. Berg Publishers, London.

1992a   Recent Archaeological and Paleoenvironmental Investigations in Southwest Florida. In *Culture and Environment in the Domain of the Calusa*, edited by W. H. Marquardt, pp. 9-57. Institute of Archaeology and Paleoenvironmental Studies, Monograph 1. University of Florida, Gainesville.

1992b   Shell Artifacts from the Caloosahatchee Area. In *Culture and Environment in the Domain of the Calusa*, edited by W. H. Marquardt, pp. 191-227. Institute of Archaeology and Paleoenvironmental Studies, Monograph 1. University of Florida, Gainesville.

1995   (editor) *The Archaeology of Useppa Island*. Institute of Archaeology and Paleoenvironmental Studies, Monograph 3. University of Florida, Gainesville. (in preparation)

Neill, Wilfred T.

1955   The Identity of Florida's "Spanish Indians." *The Florida Anthropologist* 8:43-57.

Newsom, Lee A.

1989   *Paleoethnobotany of Windover (8BR246): An Archaic Period Mortuary Site in Central Florida*. Paper presented at the 53rd annual meeting of the Society for American Archaeology, Phoenix, Arizona.

Parks, Arva Moore

1985   *Where the River Found the Bay: Historical Study of the Granada Site*. Archaeology and History of the Granada Site, Volume 2. John W. Griffin, general editor. Florida Division of Archives, History, and Records Management, Tallahassee, Florida.

Quitmyer, Irvy R. and Douglas S. Jones

1992   Calendars of the Coast: Seasonal Growth Increment Patterns in Shells of Modern and Archaeological Southern Quahogs, *Mercenaria campechiensis*, from Charlotte Harbor, Florida. In *Culture and Environment in the Domain of the Calusa*, edited by W. H. Marquardt, pp. 247-264. Institute of Archaeology and Paleoenvironmental Studies, Monograph 1. University of Florida, Gainesville.

Romans, Bernard

1775   *The Natural History of Florida*. Facsimile reproduction, 1962, of the 1775 edition. University Presses of Florida, Gainesville.

Russo, Michael

1991   *Final Report on Horr's Island: The Archaeology of Archaic and Glades Settlement and Subsistence Patterns* (with chapters by Ann Cordell, Lee Newsom, and Sylvia Scudder). Report submitted to Key Marco Developments by the

Florida Museum of Natural History, Gainesville, Florida.   Copy on file, Florida Museum of Natural History, Gainesville.

Scarry, C. Margaret and Lee A. Newsom

1992   Archaeobotanical Research in the Calusa Heartland.   In *Culture and Environment in the Domain of the Calusa*, edited by W. H. Marquardt, pp. 375-401.   Institute of Archaeology and Paleoenvironmental Studies, Monograph 1. University of Florida, Gainesville.

Stapor, Frank W., Jr., Thomas D. Mathews, and Fonda E. Lindfors-Kearns

1991   Barrier Island Progradation and Holocene Sea-Level History in Southwest Florida.   *Journal of Coastal Research* 7(3):815-838.

Stewart, Hilary

1982   *Indian Fishing: Early Methods of the Northwest Coast*.   University of Washington Press, Seattle.

Storey, Margaret

1937   The Relationship between Normal Range and Mortality of Fishes Due to Cold at Sanibel Island, Florida.   *Ecology* 18(1):10-26.

Storey, Margaret and E. W. Gudger

1936   Mortality of Fishes Due to Cold at Sanibel Island, Florida, 1886-1936.   *Ecology* 17(4):640-648.

Swanton, John R.

1922   *Early History of the Creek Indians and their Neighbors*. Bureau of American Ethnology, Bulletin 73.   United States Government Printing Office, Washington, D.C.

Upchurch, Sam B., Pliny Jewell IV, and Eric DeHaven

1992   Stratigraphy of Indian "Mounds" in the Charlotte Harbor Area, Florida: Sea-level Rise and Paleoenvironments. In *Culture and Environment in the Domain of the Calusa*, edited by W. H. Marquardt, pp. 59-103. Institute of Archaeology and Paleoenvironmental Studies, Monograph 1. University of Florida, Gainesville.

Walker, Karen J.

1992　　　The Zooarchaeology of Charlotte Harbor's Prehistoric Maritime Adaptation: Spatial and Temporal Perspectives. In *Culture and Environment in the Domain of the Calusa*, edited by W. H. Marquardt, pp. 265-366. Institute of Archaeology and Paleoenvironmental Studies, Monograph 1. University of Florida, Gainesville.

Walker, Karen J., Frank W. Stapor, Jr., and William H. Marquardt

1994　　　Episodic Sea Levels and Human Occupation at Southwest Florida's Wightman Site. *The Florida Anthropologist* 47:161-179.

Wang, Johnson C. S. and Edward C. Raney

1971　　　*Distributions and Fluctuations in the Fish Fauna of the Charlotte Harbor Estuary, Florida.* Charlotte Harbor Estuarine Studies, Mote Marine Laboratory, New City Island, Sarasota, Florida.

Widmer, Randolph J.

1988　　　*The Evolution of the Calusa: A Non-Agricultural Chiefdom on the Southwest Florida Coast.* University of Alabama Press, Tuscaloosa and London.

Williams, John Lee

1837　　　*The Territory of Florida: Or, Sketches of the Topography, Civil and Natural History of the Country, the Climate, and the Indian Tribes from the First Discovery to the Present Time.* (Facsimile edition, 1962. University Presses of Florida, Gainesville.)

Williams, Lindsey and U. S. Cleveland

1993　　　*Our Fascinating Past: Charlotte Harbor — The Early Years.* Charlotte Harbor Area Historical Society, Punta Gorda, Florida.

Williams, Robert

1753　　　*An Account of the First Discovery and Natural History of Florida.* London, England.